6TH Edition

BEST ⛺ TENT
Camping

COLORADO

YOUR CAR-CAMPING GUIDE TO SCENIC BEAUTY, THE SOUNDS
OF NATURE, AND AN ESCAPE FROM CIVILIZATION

Monica Parpal Stockbridge
Prior editions by Johnny Molloy and Kim Lipker

MENASHA RIDGE PRESS
Your Guide to the Outdoors Since 1982
an imprint of AdventureKEEN

For Jason and River

Best Tent Camping: Colorado
Copyright © 2022 by Monica Parpal Stockbridge
Copyright © 2012, 2007, 2004, 2001 by Johnny Molloy and Kim Lipker
Copyright © 1999 by Kim Lipker
All rights reserved
Printed in the United States of America
Published by Menasha Ridge Press
Distributed by Publishers Group West
Sixth edition, first printing

Library of Congress Cataloging-in-Publication Data

Names: Stockbridge, Monica Parpal, 1983– author.
Title: Best tent camping Colorado : your car-camping guide to scenic beauty, the sounds of nature, and an escape
    from civilization / Monica Parpal Stockbridge.
Description: Sixth Edition. | Birmingham, AL : Menasha Ridge Press, [2022] | "Prior editions by Kim Lipker and
    Johnny Molloy."
Summary: "With our local camping experts on your side, the very best tent camping in your state is only a
    quick read away. Hand-selected for their appeal to tent campers who love seclusion, beauty, quiet, and
    security, the 50 campsites described in each of the Best Tent Camping guides represent the best of the best"
    —Provided by publisher.
Identifiers: LCCN 2022006480 (pbk.) | LCCN 2022006481 (ebook) | ISBN 9781634043014 (pbk.) |
    ISBN 9781634043021 (ebook)
Subjects: LCSH: Camp sites, facilities, etc.—Colorado—Guidebooks. | Camping—Colorado. |
    Colorado—Guidebooks.
Classification: LCC GV191.42.C6 M65 2022 (pbk.) | LCC GV191.42.C6 (ebook) |
    DDC 796.5409788—dc23/eng/20220405
LC record available at lccn.loc.gov/2022006480
LC ebook record available at lccn.loc.gov/2022006481

Cover design: Scott McGrew
Book design: Jonathan Norberg
Text design: Annie Long
Cartography: Steve Jones, Kim Lipker, Johnny Molloy, and Monica Parpal Stockbridge
Cover and interior photos: Monica Parpal Stockbridge, except where noted on page
Proofreader: Vanessa Rusch
Indexer: Frances Lennie

 MENASHA RIDGE PRESS
An imprint of AdventureKEEN
2204 First Ave. S., Ste. 102
Birmingham, AL 35233
800-678-7006, fax 877-374-9016

Visit menasharidge.com for a complete listing of our books and for ordering information. Contact us at our website, at
facebook.com/menasharidge, or at twitter.com/menasharidge with questions or comments. To find out more about
who we are and what we're doing, visit blog.menasharidge.com.

CONTENTS

Colorado Campground Locator Map v

Acknowledgments vi

Preface vii

Best Campgrounds ix

Map Legend xi

Introduction 1

EASTERN COLORADO 13

1 Jackson Lake State Park Campground 14

2 John Martin Reservoir State Wildlife Area: Lake Hasty and
The Point Campgrounds 17

3 Pawnee National Grassland: Crow Valley Family Campground 21

4 South Republican State Wildlife Area Dispersed Camping 24

NORTH CENTRAL COLORADO 27

5 Buffalo Campground 28

6 The Crags Campground 31

7 Elbert Creek Campground 34

8 Pinewood Reservoir Campground 37

9 Gold Park Campground 40

10 Golden Gate Canyon State Park Campgrounds 43

11 Guanella Pass Campground 46

12 Hermit Park Open Space: Hermit's Hollow Campground 49

13 Rocky Mountain National Park: Longs Peak Campground 52

14 Lost Park Campground 55

15 The Narrows Campgrounds: Lower 58

16 Peaceful Valley and Camp Dick Campgrounds 61

17 Rainbow Lakes Campground 65

18 Robbers Roost Campground 68

19 Rocky Mountain National Park: Aspenglen Campground 71

20 Weston Pass Campground 74

21 Staunton State Park Campground 77

NORTHWEST COLORADO 80

22 Cold Springs Campground 81

23 Colorado National Monument: Saddlehorn Campground 84

24 Dinosaur National Monument: Echo Park Campground 87

25 Fulford Cave Campground 90

26 Irish Canyon Campground 93

27 Rifle Falls State Park Campground 96

28 Shepherds Rim Campground 99

29 Pearl Lake State Park Campground 102

30 Weir and Johnson Campground. 105

SOUTH CENTRAL COLORADO 108

31 Alvarado Campground 109

32 Bear Lake Campground. 112

33 Great Sand Dunes National Park & Preserve:
Piñon Flats Campground 115

34 East Ridge Campground 118

35 O'Haver Lake Campground 121

36 Mueller State Park Campground 124

37 North Crestone Creek Campground 127

38 Trujillo Meadows Campground 130

SOUTHWEST COLORADO 133

39 Black Canyon of the Gunnison National Park:
North Rim Campground. 134

40 Burro Bridge Campground 137

41 Cathedral Campground. 140

42 Lost Lake Campground 143

43 Lost Trail Campground 146

44 Mesa Verde National Park: Morefield Campground 149

45 Mirror Lake Campground 152

46 Ridgway State Park Campgrounds 155

47 Silver Jack Campground 158

48 Amphitheater Campground. 161

49 Stone Cellar Campground. 164

50 Transfer Park Campground 166

Appendix A: Camping Equipment Checklist 170

Appendix B: Sources of Information 171

Index 173

About the Authors 178

Colorado Campground Locator Map

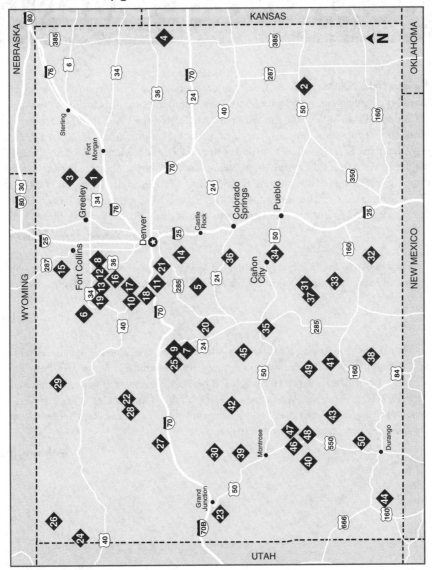

ACKNOWLEDGMENTS

My heartfelt thanks go to the many park rangers, camp hosts, and fellow campers who shared their information and passion for these campgrounds. This includes the employees at Colorado Parks & Wildlife, the National Park Service, the U.S. Forest Service, and Rocky Mountain Recreation Company. Specifically, thanks to John Anarella, Mike Brown, Destiny Chapman, Sami Colvin, Jeremiah Martinez, Jack Mudd, Michael Petrarca, Duane Stegner, Jeffer Wingate, and Crystal Young. Many thanks to my supportive friends, family, and camping buddies, including Mindy Sink, Melissa Markle, Sarah Young, the DMAC crew, Carie Behounek, Christie Aschwanden, the Barbers, Lucy Beaugard, Eleanor and Vern Stockbridge, and Jacqueline and Marc Parpal. Most of all, thanks to my husband, Jason.

—Monica Parpal Stockbridge

I would like to thank Johnny Molloy; the folks at Menasha Ridge Press; my friends and my family; and the helpful folks at the National Park Service, the U.S. Forest Service, and Colorado Parks & Wildlife.

—Kim Lipker

Thanks to the following for their help with the original editions of the guide: Joe Mayer; Sam Berry; Becky Anderson; Kate Brannan; Paul Welschinger; Susan Webster; Margaret Albrecht; Bryan Delay; James Herbaugh; Pat Molloy; Bill Armstrong; Keith Stinnett; Bryan Hatfield; Michael and Nan Wolfenbarger; Nelle Molloy; Larry of Castle Rock; Beverly, Wilbert, and Craig Spieker of Castle Rock, who made me feel at home; Regi Roberts; John Cox; and David Zaczyk, master of the semicolon.

—Johnny Molloy

PREFACE

I took on the exciting and daunting task of updating *Best Tent Camping: Colorado* in mid-2019. I was determined to bring readers up to speed on what's been changed, improved, and upgraded in the Colorado tent camping scene since this book was last published 10 years ago.

After exploring nearly two dozen campgrounds in 2019, I had big plans to spend all of summer 2020 camping. Then, two things happened. I found out I was expecting my first child. A few months later, a global pandemic upended life as we knew it.

Even as I was gearing up to visit campgrounds with my face mask and maternity pillow in tow, a statewide stay-at-home order doused my plans. Many state and national parks weren't open to visitors that summer. Furthermore, Colorado suffered through the three largest wildfires in state history that year, scarring over 400,000 acres and affecting multiple communities, not to mention a few of the campgrounds previously included in this book.

Fast-forward two years. My child is thriving, and things in Colorado are looking a little more hopeful. My family and I spent much of 2021 adjusting to a whole lot of "new normals," and we were very fortunate to spend a lot of time outdoors.

Most of the campgrounds listed in the previous editions of this book remain here within these pages, edited and updated to the best of my ability with the latest maps and logistical information. For this latest edition, we've also added color photos to help reveal some of the beauty each area has to offer. A few places were removed, due to either wildfire scarring, downed trees from mountain pine beetle infestation, or simply my preference for a more desirable spot. Generally speaking, I aimed to continue the original authors' intention: giving the reader opportunities for a great camping experience near some of the state's most incredible natural features and historic locations.

One major update is that all Colorado state parks now require reservations for camping. This new measure has faced mixed reactions: A reservation can be a nice guarantee you'll have a spot in a time when outdoor recreation is gaining more popularity. Yet the booking process can be tedious. You'll need to think several months ahead, have internet or phone access, and act fast to get your preferred spot. There are still several campgrounds in this book that are fully or partially first come, first served, and a few that let you camp for free.

Looking back, this project gave me the chance to make some very special memories during a difficult time. My friend Carie and I hoofed it all the way up the hill at Staunton State Park Campground, then drank wine while watching a spectacular sunset. My friend Sarah made me a boil-in-a-bag omelet after a night spent at Golden Gate National Park Campground. My husband and I took our daughter on her first camping trip to Crow Valley Campground at Pawnee National Grassland, spoon-feeding her under a symphony of birdsong while my in-laws tended the campfire. My parents and I dipped our feet in Medano Creek at Great Sand Dunes National Park, and looked up in awe at the Milky Way from Alvarado Campground near Westcliffe.

A few of the people I met while exploring these campsites gently suggested that I leave their favorite campgrounds out of the book. They are concerned that, like many of Colorado's most iconic places, they could be "loved to death." Rightly so. The journey of updating this book was a stark reminder that it's a privilege to be able to experience these awe-inspiring outdoor places, which are both rugged and fragile. Consider the next camper when you leave your site, and leave it better than when you arrived. Always make sure campfires are out cold before you leave or go to sleep for the night. Stash your food where bears and other wildlife can't get to it. Be courteous, clean, and careful, and maybe we can make these special places last for years to come.

Camping in a tent is, I think, one of the best ways to get connected with nature—and with each other. I hope you'll take the opportunity to try it, and I hope you'll take this guidebook with you when you do.

—Monica Parpal Stockbridge

The Uncompahgre River runs alongside Pa-Co-Chu-Puk Campground at Ridgway State Park (see page 155).

BEST CAMPGROUNDS

BEST FOR PRIVACY

6 The Crags Campground **North Central Colorado** (p. 31)

12 Hermit Park Open Space: Hermit's Hollow Campground **North Central Colorado** (p. 49)

21 Staunton State Park Campground **North Central Colorado** (p. 77)

24 Dinosaur National Monument: Echo Park Campground **Northwest Colorado** (p. 87)

37 North Crestone Creek Campground **South Central Colorado** (p. 127)

BEST FOR SPACIOUSNESS

1 Jackson Lake State Park Campground **Eastern Colorado** (p. 14)

17 Rainbow Lakes Campground **North Central Colorado** (p. 65)

26 Irish Canyon Campground **Northwest Colorado** (p. 93)

34 East Ridge Campground **South Central Colorado** (p. 118)

40 Burro Bridge Campground **Southwest Colorado** (p. 137)

BEST FOR QUIET

6 The Crags Campground **North Central Colorado** (p. 31)

17 Rainbow Lakes Campground **North Central Colorado** (p. 65)

24 Dinosaur National Monument: Echo Park Campground **Northwest Colorado** (p. 87)

40 Burro Bridge Campground **Southwest Colorado** (p. 137)

43 Lost Trail Campground **Southwest Colorado** (p. 146)

BEST FOR SECURITY

19 Rocky Mountain National Park: Aspenglen Campground **North Central Colorado** (p. 71)

23 Colorado National Monument: Saddlehorn Campground **Northwest Colorado** (p. 84)

27 Rifle Falls State Park Campground **Northwest Colorado** (p. 96)

29 Pearl Lake State Park Campground **Northwest Colorado** (p. 102)

36 Mueller State Park Campground **South Central Colorado** (p. 124)

BEST FOR CLEANLINESS

21 Staunton State Park Campground **North Central Colorado** (p. 77)

36 Mueller State Park Campground **South Central Colorado** (p. 124)

40 Burro Bridge Campground **Southwest Colorado** (p. 137)

44 Mesa Verde National Park: Morefield Campground **Southwest Colorado** (p. 149)

46 Ridgway State Park Campgrounds **Southwest Colorado** (p. 155)

BEST FOR WHEELCHAIR ACCESSIBILITY

3 Pawnee National Grassland: Crow Valley Family Campground **Eastern Colorado** (p. 21)

8 Pinewood Reservoir Campground **North Central Colorado** (p. 37)

16 Peaceful Valley and Camp Dick Campgrounds **North Central Colorado** (p. 61)

19 Rocky Mountain National Park: Aspenglen Campground **North Central Colorado** (p. 71)

33 Great Sand Dunes National Park and Preserve: Piñon Flats Campground
South Central Colorado (p. 115)

BEST CAMPING NEAR A LAKE

8 Pinewood Reservoir Campground **North Central Colorado** (p. 37)

17 Rainbow Lakes Campground **North Central Colorado** (p. 65)

29 Pearl Lake State Park Campground **Northwest Colorado** (p. 102)

42 Lost Lake Campground **Southwest Colorado** (p. 143)

46 Ridgway State Park Campgrounds **Southwest Colorado** (p. 155)

BEST FOR GREAT VIEWS

23 Colorado National Monument: Saddlehorn Campground **Northwest Colorado** (p. 84)

28 Shepherds Rim Campground **Northwest Colorado** (p. 99)

39 Black Canyon of the Gunnison National Park: North Rim Campground
Southwest Colorado (p. 134)

46 Ridgway State Park Campgrounds **Southwest Colorado** (p. 155)

48 Amphitheater Campground **Southwest Colorado** (p. 161)

Map Legend

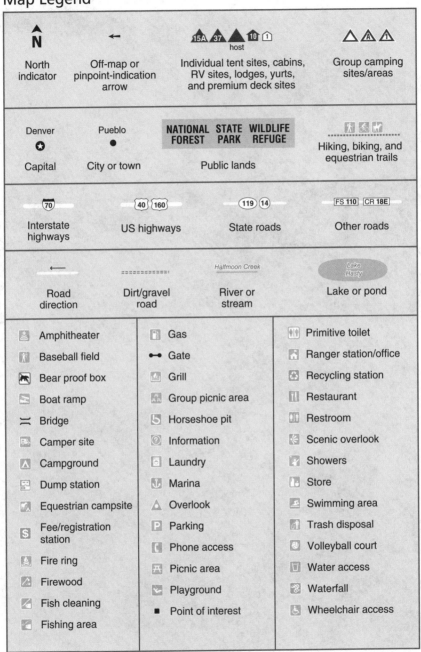

N North indicator	← Off-map or pinpoint-indication arrow	15A 37 ▲ 10 1 host Individual tent sites, cabins, RV sites, lodges, yurts, and premium deck sites	△ ⚠ ⚠ Group camping sites/areas
Denver ✪ Capital	Pueblo ● City or town	NATIONAL STATE WILDLIFE FOREST PARK REFUGE Public lands	Hiking, biking, and equestrian trails
70 Interstate highways	40 160 US highways	119 14 State roads	FS 110 CR 18E Other roads
← Road direction	Dirt/gravel road	Halfmoon Creek River or stream	Lake Hasty Lake or pond

Amphitheater	Gas	Primitive toilet
Baseball field	Gate	Ranger station/office
Bear proof box	Grill	Recycling station
Boat ramp	Group picnic area	Restaurant
Bridge	Horseshoe pit	Restroom
Camper site	Information	Scenic overlook
Campground	Laundry	Showers
Dump station	Marina	Store
Equestrian campsite	Overlook	Swimming area
Fee/registration station	Parking	Trash disposal
Fire ring	Phone access	Volleyball court
Firewood	Picnic area	Water access
Fish cleaning	Playground	Waterfall
Fishing area	Point of interest	Wheelchair access

Fancy Lake near Gold Park Campground (see page 40)

INTRODUCTION

ABOUT THIS BOOK AND COLORADO TENT CAMPING

Welcome to the sixth edition of Best Tent Camping: Colorado. If you're new to tent camping or even if you're a seasoned camper, take a few minutes to read the following introduction, which explains how this book is organized and how to use it.

CAMPGROUND PROFILES

Each profile contains a concise but informative narrative of the campground, as well as individual sites. This descriptive text is enhanced with at-a-glance ratings and information, GPS-based trailhead coordinates, and accurate driving directions that lead you from a major road to the parking area most convenient to the trailhead. On the first page of each profile is a ratings box.

THE RATING SYSTEM

This book includes a rating system for Colorado's 50 best tent campgrounds. Six campground attributes—beauty, privacy, spaciousness, quiet, security, and cleanliness—are ranked using a five-star system. A low rating in one or two areas, especially privacy and spaciousness, was not necessarily grounds for exclusion from this book. In some cases, the nature of the terrain just doesn't allow for big, private sites, yet the campground still may be well worth a visit. This system should help you find what you are looking for.

★★★★★ The site is **ideal** in that category.

★★★★ The site is **exemplary** in that category.

★★★ The site is **very good** in that category.

★★ The site is **above average** in that category.

★ The site is **acceptable** in that category.

BEAUTY

In judging beauty, we took into account both what the general area has to offer and the campground. The most beautiful campgrounds have sites that you just don't want to leave and locations with easy access to breathtaking scenery.

PRIVACY

Privacy is determined by how much your neighbors can pay attention to what you are doing and vice versa. The best campgrounds have plenty of green space (shrubs and trees) between adjoining sites, as well as staggered sites (that is, the entrance to the site across the road is not directly opposite yours).

SPACIOUSNESS

While this category contributes to the amount of privacy you have, it refers mostly to how much space you have to move around in. The sites at some campgrounds are surprisingly large—to the point of overkill; others are incredibly small.

QUIET

Our evaluations were influenced to a great extent by the presence of RVs and the kinds of visitors a park tends to get (campgrounds near urban areas, for example, are usually a bit noisy, as are those that cater to families with children). We also considered the extent to which you could get away from the fray at a particular campground. You can expect some variation within our ratings based on whether you visit a campground during the week or on a weekend; on holiday weekends, all bets are off.

SECURITY

With few exceptions, we've found Colorado campgrounds to be very safe and secure, due largely to the presence of campground hosts and park rangers making the rounds. The only places at which we felt security might be compromised were those remote campgrounds that saw few visitors and had no host or ranger on duty.

CLEANLINESS

Our judgments were based on the presence and remnants of past campers around the campsite (trash, tent stakes, burned logs, etc.) and on the restroom facilities. We did take into account that primitive toilets tend to be a little less tidy than modern facilities, although there seemed to us to be little reason for either to be a mess.

CAMPGROUND LOCATOR MAP AND MAP LEGEND

Use the locator map on page v to assess the location of each campground. The campground's number also appears in the table of contents and on the profile's first page. The book is organized by region, as indicated in the table of contents. A map legend that details the symbols found on the campground layout maps appears on page xi.

CAMPGROUND-LAYOUT MAPS

Each profile contains a campground-layout map that includes campground sites, internal roads, facilities, and at least one major road leading into the area.

CAMPGROUND-ENTRANCE GPS COORDINATES

This book includes GPS coordinates for each campground. Topographic maps show latitude and longitude, as well as UTM grid lines. The survey datum used to arrive at the coordinates in this book is WGS84 (versus NAD27 or WGS83). The latitude and longitude coordinates may be entered into a GPS unit, whether handheld or on a vehicle. Just make sure your GPS unit is set to navigate using the WGS84 datum. Now you can navigate directly to the campground. Readers can also easily find each campground in this book by using the directions provided.

WEATHER

Weather in Colorado can change every 10 minutes. Be prepared for anything: sun, snow, flash flooding, lightning, hail, and even tornadoes. Start by knowing the weather forecast and the road conditions; then pack smart. It can be a lovely day in Denver, but a campground may be inaccessible due to blizzard conditions. You must be prepared, and you should consider carrying a hiking card (CORSAR, discussed on page 4). If you need to be rescued, these cards can save your life and your pocketbook.

CLIMATE OVERVIEW

- Semiarid
- Dry summers
- Short springs
- Mild winters except in the mountains

AVERAGE TEMPERATURE BY MONTH: DENVER AREA						
	JAN	**FEB**	**MAR**	**APR**	**MAY**	**JUN**
HIGH	47°F	49°F	56°F	62°F	72°F	81°F
LOW	16°F	18°F	25°F	33°F	42°F	50°F
	JUL	**AUG**	**SEP**	**OCT**	**NOV**	**DEC**
HIGH	88°F	86°F	78°F	66°F	54°F	46°F
LOW	56°F	54°F	44°F	33°F	23°F	16°F

Source: denver.org/about-denver/resources/weather

It is hard to generalize the climate and the altitude throughout Colorado, but we *can* tell you that what you pack and how you deal with the altitude can make or break a trip.

The Rockies' rugged and varied geography creates a number of weather zones. Whatever the region, whatever the season, be sure to dress in layers. In the summer, expect warm days and cool evenings. Bring shorts, hiking boots, a sweater, and a weatherproof jacket. In the winter, bring snow gear for the mountains and warm outerwear for elsewhere.

ALTITUDE SICKNESS

Nothing ruins an outing more often than altitude sickness. The illness is usually characterized by shortness of breath, extreme headache, lightheadedness, sleeplessness, vomiting, and an overall sick feeling. Our advice: take it easy. When traveling to higher altitude, where there is less oxygen, hotter sun, and lower air pressure, give your body a day or two to adjust. Consider spending a night in Denver before heading up to the high country. Drink plenty of water, and lay off drinking and smoking. Wear sunglasses and sunscreen. As always, if serious symptoms persist, locate the nearest emergency room, or call 911.

LIGHTNING AND TORNADOES

Violent storms are common in June, July, and August. If you are caught in a lightning storm above treeline, stay off ridgetops, spread out if you are in a group, and squat or sit on a foam pad with your feet together. Keep away from rock outcroppings and isolated trees. If someone has been struck, be prepared to use CPR to help restore breathing and heartbeat.

In the event of a tornado (they are extremely common in the eastern portion of Colorado), immediately seek shelter. If you are in an open field, lie down in the nearest ditch.

SEARCH-AND-RESCUE CARDS

The Colorado Outdoor Recreation Search and Rescue (CORSAR) card may be purchased at most outdoor shops, such as REI, or online at colorado.gov/sar. You can pay $3 for a one-year card or $12 for a five-year card. CORSAR is not insurance—it does not pay for medical transportation, which may include ambulances or helicopter flights. The card does allow prompt reimbursement to county sheriffs for costs involved in a search-and-rescue mission (if the subject of a search does *not* have a card, the reimbursement request is held until the end of the year and funds are disbursed only if available). These expenses can include mileage, meals, equipment, gasoline, and rental fees (horses, ATVs, aircraft) for vehicles used in the search. By purchasing a card, you help ensure that, should you become lost or in need of rescue, the search-and-rescue teams who respond have sufficient training and equipment and will not have to personally incur expense due to your emergency.

FIRST AID KIT

A typical first aid kit may contain more items than you might think necessary. These are just the basics. Prepackaged kits in waterproof bags are available (Atwater Carey and Adventure Medical make a variety of such kits). As a preventive measure, take along sunscreen and insect repellent. Even though there are quite a few items in the following list, they pack down into a small space:

- Ace bandages
- Adhesive bandages
- Antibiotic ointment (Neosporin or the generic equivalent)
- Antiseptic or disinfectant, such as Betadine or hydrogen peroxide
- Aspirin or acetaminophen
- Benadryl or the generic equivalent, diphenhydramine (for allergic reactions)
- Butterfly-closure bandages
- Epinephrine autoinjector (for severe allergic reactions to bee stings)
- Gauze (one roll)
- Gauze compresses (six 4 x 4–inch pads)
- Moleskin or other blister patches, such as Spenco 2nd Skin
- Tweezers
- Waterproof first aid tape
- Waterproof matches and/or pocket lighter
- Whistle (it's more effective in signaling rescuers than your voice is)

ANIMAL AND PLANT HAZARDS

BLACK BEARS

There are no definite rules about what to do if you meet a bear. In most cases the bear will detect you first and leave. Avoid dangerous situations by camping and hiking in groups, and carry bear pepper spray if you'll be in the backcountry. If you do encounter a bear, here are some suggestions from the National Park Service:

- Stay calm. If you're with small children, pick them up immediately.
- Remain still, talking calmly to alert the bear to your presence and identify you as a human.
- If the bear is stationary, move away slowly and sideways while keeping an eye on the bear.
- Make yourself appear larger.
- Give the bear plenty of room to leave; bears will rarely attack unless they are threatened.
- Don't run or make sudden movements; running may provoke the bear, and you cannot outrun one.
- Do not attempt to climb trees to escape bears, as they are excellent climbers.
- Fight back if you are attacked. Black bears have been driven away when people have fought back with rocks, sticks, binoculars, and even their bare hands.

MOUNTAIN LIONS

Mountain lion attacks on people are rare, with fewer than 12 fatalities in 100 years. If you find yourself in mountain lion territory, stay alert—especially at dawn or dusk when mountain lions are most active. Keep children and pets close, and never approach a mountain lion. Here are more suggestions from the National Park Service:

- Stay calm, and talk firmly to the lion.
- Move slowly.
- Back up or stop; never crouch down or turn your back to retrieve items.
- Never run because lions will chase and attack.
- Raise your arms. If you are wearing a sweater or coat; hold it open wide.
- Pick up children and make them appear larger.
- If the lion becomes aggressive, throw rocks and large objects at it. This is the time to convince the lion that you are not prey and are a danger to it.
- If you are attacked, fight back and try to remain standing.

MOOSE

Moose are spectacular to see in the wild. They are larger than life, standing up to 6 feet tall at the shoulder and weighing up to 1,400 pounds. But moose are best viewed from a distance, as they are extremely dangerous. If a moose hasn't detected you yet, keep it that way. Here are more tips from the National Park Service:

- If you see a moose, stay calm.
- If it knows you're there, talk to it softly and move away slowly. You want to convince the moose that you aren't a threat.
- Be especially careful around cow moose with their young.
- If you think a moose is going to charge you, run away and take cover behind a tree or car.
- If a moose knocks you down, curl up in a ball, protect your head with your arms, and keep still. Fighting back will only convince the moose that you may still be a threat.

TICKS

Ticks like to hang out in the brush that grows around campsites and along trails. Their numbers seem to explode in the hot summer months, but you should be tick-aware year-round. The ticks that light onto you will be very small, sometimes so tiny you won't be able to spot them. Primarily of two varieties, deer ticks and dog ticks, both need a few hours of actual attachment before they can transmit any disease they may harbor. Ticks may settle in shoes, socks, and hats and may take several hours to actually latch on. The best strategy is to visually check yourself a couple of times a day, especially after a walk in the woods. Ticks that haven't attached are easily removed but not easily killed. If you pick off a tick in the woods, just toss it aside. If you find one on your body at camp, you may want to dispatch it (otherwise, it may find you again). For ticks that are embedded, removal with tweezers is best.

Deer tick

Jim Gathany/Centers for Disease Control and Prevention (public domain)

SNAKES

Spend some time in Colorado and you may be surprised by the variety of snakes in the area. Most snake encounters will be with garter snakes, water snakes, and bull snakes (while not venomous, they are rather large and scary-looking). The only venomous snake in the region is the rattlesnake. Rattler sightings are very common. A good rule of thumb is to give rattlers a wide berth and leave them alone. In the event you are bitten, remain calm, stay as still as possible, and get help immediately.

POISON IVY

Recognizing poison ivy and avoiding contact with it is the most effective way to prevent the painful, itchy rashes associated with these plants. In the West, poison ivy is found as a small plant with three leaflets to a leaf. Yet, the plant can grow up to 5 feet high in certain areas. Remember "leaves of three, let them be." Urushiol, the oil in the sap of these plants, is responsible for the rash. Usually within 12–14 hours of exposure, raised lines and/or blisters will appear, accompanied by a terrible itch. Refrain from scratching because bacteria under fingernails can cause infection and you could spread the rash to other parts of your body. Wash and dry the rash thoroughly, applying calamine lotion or another product to help dry the rash. If itching or blistering is severe, seek medical attention. Remember that oil can remain on contaminated clothes, pets, and hiking gear and reinfect you or someone else, so wash not only any exposed parts of your body but also clothes, pets, and gear.

Poison ivy

Tom Watson

MOSQUITOES

Although it's not a common occurrence, individuals can contract the West Nile virus after being bitten by an infected mosquito. *Culex* mosquitoes, the primary variety that can transmit the virus to humans, thrive in urban rather than natural areas. They lay their eggs in stagnant water and can breed in any standing water that remains for more than five days.

Most people infected with West Nile virus have no symptoms, but some may become ill, usually 3–15 days after being bitten. In Colorado, August and September are the high-risk periods for West Nile virus. At this time of year—and anytime you expect mosquitoes to be buzzing around—you may want to wear protective clothing, such as long sleeves, long pants, and socks. Loose-fitting, light-colored clothing is best. Spray clothing with insect repellent. Remember to follow the instructions on the repellent carefully, and take extra care with children.

CAMPING ETIQUETTE

Camping experiences can vary wildly depending on a variety of factors, such as weather, preparedness, fellow campers, and time of year. Here are a few tips on how to create good vibes with fellow campers and wildlife you encounter.

- **OBTAIN ALL PERMITS AND AUTHORIZATION AS REQUIRED.** Make sure you check in, pay your fee, and mark your site as directed. Don't make the mistake of grabbing a seemingly empty site that looks more appealing than your site. It could be reserved. If you are unhappy with the site you've been assigned, check with the campground host for other options.

- **LEAVE ONLY FOOTPRINTS.** Be sensitive to the ground beneath you. Be sure to place all garbage in designated receptacles, or pack it out if no receptacle is available. No one likes to see the trash someone else has left behind.

- **NEVER SPOOK ANIMALS.** It's common for animals to wander through campsites, where they may be accustomed to the presence of humans (and our food). An unannounced approach, a sudden movement, or a loud noise startles most animals. A surprised animal can be dangerous to you, to others, and to itself. Give them plenty of space.

- **PLAN AHEAD.** Know your equipment, your ability, and the area in which you are camping—and prepare accordingly. Be self-sufficient at all times; carry necessary supplies for changes in weather or other conditions. A well-executed trip is a satisfaction to you and to others.

- **BE COURTEOUS** to hikers, bikers, and other campers you encounter—even RVers.

- **STRICTLY FOLLOW THE CAMPGROUND'S RULES** regarding the building of fires. If there's a fire ban, go without a campfire that night. If you are allowed to build a fire, never burn trash; trash smoke smells terrible, and trash debris left in a fire pit or grill is unsightly.

TIPS FOR A HAPPY CAMPING TRIP

Having a bad camping trip is no fun, but it happens from time to time. Preparation and flexibility are key. To assist with making your outing a happy one, here are some pointers:

- Reserve your site ahead of time, especially if it's a weekend or holiday, or if the campground is wildly popular. Many prime campgrounds require at least a six-month lead time on reservations. Check before you go. If you are aiming for first-come, first-served camping, have a backup campground in mind in case all the campsites are full when you arrive.

- Pick your camping buddies wisely. A family trip is pretty straightforward, but be prepared if you're inviting grumpy Uncle Fred who doesn't like bugs, sunshine, or marshmallows. Make sure all campers are on the same page regarding expectations of difficulty, sleeping arrangements, and food requirements.

- Don't duplicate equipment, such as cooking pots and lanterns, among campers in your party. Carry what you need to have a good time, but don't turn the trip into a major moving experience.

- Dress appropriately for the season. Educate yourself on the highs and lows of the specific area you plan to visit (see page 3). It may be warm at night in the summer in your backyard, but up in the mountains it will be quite chilly.

- Pitch your tent on a level surface, and place it on a tarp or specially designed footprint to thwart ground moisture and protect the tent floor. Do a little site maintenance, such as picking up small rocks and sticks that can damage your tent floor and make sleep uncomfortable.

- Stake down your tent as soon as you pitch it, as rogue winds can easily topple a tent. Keep your rain fly handy in case of sudden rainstorms.

- Pack a sleeping pad to make sleeping on the ground more comfortable. Take one that is full-length and thicker than you think you might need. This will not only keep your hips from aching on the hard ground but will also help keep you warm. If you camp with an air mattress, be sure to place a sleeping pad between it and your sleeping bag to provide a buffer between all that cold air and you.

- If you are not hiking to a primitive campsite, there is no need to skimp on food due to weight. Plan hot, tasty meals and bring everything you will need to prepare, cook, eat, and clean up afterward.

- If you're prone to using the bathroom multiple times at night, you should plan ahead. Keep a headlamp or flashlight and any other accoutrements you may need by the tent door, and know exactly where you're going.

- Standing dead trees and storm-damaged living trees can pose a real hazard to tent campers. These trees may have loose or broken limbs that could fall at any time. When choosing a spot to rest or a backcountry campsite, look up.

BACKCOUNTRY CAMPING ADVICE

Be sure to check whether a permit is required before entering the backcountry to camp, and practice Leave No Trace camping ethics (visit lnt.org for details). Adhere to the adages "Pack it in; pack it out" and "Take only pictures. Leave only footprints."

Open fires are permitted except during dry times when the U.S. Forest Service may issue a fire ban. Backpacking stoves are strongly encouraged.

You are required to hang your food away from bears and other animals. Not only does this help prevent potentially dangerous human–wildlife encounters, but it also keeps wildlife from being introduced to and becoming dependent on human food, which can happen as they learn to associate backpacks and backpackers with food. Make sure you have about 40 feet of thin but sturdy rope to properly secure your food bag. Ideally, you should throw your rope over a stout limb that extends 10 or more feet above the ground. Make sure the rope hangs at least 5 feet away from the tree trunk.

Solid human waste must be buried in a hole at least 3 inches deep and at least 200 feet away from trails and water sources; a trowel is basic backpacking equipment.

Following the above guidelines will increase your chances for a pleasant, safe, and low-impact interaction with nature.

VENTURING AWAY FROM THE CAMPGROUND

If you go for a hike, bike, or other excursion into the wilderness, here are some tips:

- Always carry food and water, whether you are planning to go overnight or not. Food will give you energy, help keep you warm, and sustain you in an emergency situation until help arrives. You never know if there will be a stream nearby when you become thirsty. Bring potable water or the means to treat found water. Boil or filter all found water.

- Stay on designated trails. Most hikers get lost when they leave the path. Even on clearly marked trails, there is usually a point where you have to stop and consider which direction to go. If you get disoriented, don't panic. As soon as you think you may be off-track, stop, assess your current direction, and then retrace your steps back to the point where you went awry. If you become absolutely unsure of how to continue, return to your vehicle the way you came in. Should you become completely lost and have no idea how to return to the trailhead, remaining in place along the trail and waiting for help is most often the best option for adults and always the best option for children.

- Be especially careful when crossing streams. Whether you are fording the stream or crossing on a log, make every step count. If you have any doubt about maintaining your balance on a foot log, go ahead and ford the stream instead. When fording a stream, use a trekking pole or stout stick for balance, and face upstream as you cross. If a stream seems too deep to ford, turn back. Whatever is on the other side is not worth risking your life.

- Be careful at scenic overlooks. While these areas provide spectacular views, they are potentially hazardous. Stay back from the edge of outcrops and be absolutely sure of your footing; a misstep can mean a nasty and possibly fatal fall.

- Know the symptoms of hypothermia. Shivering and forgetfulness are the two most common indicators of this insidious killer. Hypothermia can occur at any elevation, even in the summer, especially when the hiker is wearing lightweight cotton clothing, which loses its insulating properties as it absorbs moisture from perspiration. If symptoms arise, get the victim shelter, hot liquids, and dry clothes or a dry sleeping bag.

- Stay cool and collected. Your brain is the most important piece of equipment you'll need on the trail. Think before you act. Watch your step. Plan ahead. Avoiding accidents is the best recipe for a rewarding and relaxing hike.

CAMPING WITH CHILDREN

I got to experience my first taste of camping with kids as I was updating this guidebook. I took my baby on her first tent camping trip when she was 10 months old. What a fun—and exhausting—experience!

Preparing to go camping with babies or young children can be daunting, but it can also be a great way to introduce young people to the outdoors. It's a wonderful adventure and an even better family-bonding experience. It's time away from laundry, electronic devices, and school—just you and the kids and nature. Sure, it's a lot of work. But the memories you'll make, and the distraction-free together time, are priceless.

WHAT TO BRING

Packing for the kids is much like packing for the parents. Giving everyone their own duffel can help you all stay organized. When it comes to packing clothes, focus on bringing multiple layers and avoiding cotton. Instead, opt for wool or synthetics, which wick moisture away from the body and dry faster. Make sure children have multiple pairs of socks and one sturdy pair of shoes. Opt for wool socks over cotton because cotton retains moisture and may lead to blisters.

For the family, it's a good idea to pack the U.S. Forest Service's 10 Essentials: map, compass, water, knife, waterproof matches, high-energy food, extra clothing (including raingear), signal mirror, first aid kit, and whistle. Of these, pack each kid their own raingear and their own whistle, which is more effective than yelling if they happen to get lost.

Additionally, pack plenty of wholesome snacks, a water bottle for your child, sun protection (hat, sunglasses, and sunscreen), kid-friendly activities (see page 11 for some ideas), a special stuffed animal, and a book or two for bedtime. Baby wipes come in handy no matter your child's age.

Each child needs a sleeping bag that will fit his or her body and provide enough warmth at night. Do your research on sizes and temperature ratings.

If you're bringing your baby camping (and you should!), prepare to be extra flexible. Your routines may shift for a night or two, and that's OK. Bring a big tent and a portable crib, play yard, or bassinet to provide a safe place for your baby to sleep or play. If you're formula feeding, be sure you have a source of clean, potable water and a way to wash and sanitize bottles. Baby food in jars or pouches makes eating on the go super easy. A wearable baby carrier and a portable camping high chair help as well.

SAFETY CONSIDERATIONS

Children should be taught from the get-go that they must stay within eyesight of an adult. Not only could they get lost or injured, but they could also cause damage to the ecosystem. Teach your kids to treat the outdoors with respect. Also, teach children to stay where they are if they get lost. Many children relate to hugging a tree when lost—instruct them to find one, hold on, and blow their whistle. Three whistle blows is the standard distress signal, indicating "I am lost" or "I need help." Never let kids go near steep cliffs or other drop-offs. Rules about rivers and other water sources and climbing on rocks must be addressed as well. For many parents, the simple rule is "don't do it." If you bring kid-friendly distractions

The author sets up camp with her family at Transfer Park Campground (see page 166).

like binoculars, wildflower guides, or a hiking scavenger hunt, you can focus on having fun without imposing too many restrictions.

Always teach outdoor etiquette: leave no trace, pick up after yourself, and don't pick or pull anything. And, of course, "Leaves of three, let them be."

KEEP IT FUN

When camping with kids, the most important thing is to keep it fun. Planning ahead, staying flexible, and being optimistic are all key elements of a fun trip.

Before going camping away from home, plan a simple overnight in your backyard, if you have one. This can be a fun diversion for kids and serve as a dry run for parents to test out equipment, double-check gear lists, and get a sense of how kids will react to a night in a tent.

When it comes to your actual camping trip, have the kids help with planning and packing. Make a special kid-friendly map of the campground area that they can keep in their bag. Making maps helps teach direction and creativity. Create a legend with items like waterfalls, trails, trees, and tents. Have the child bring markers or crayons to mark points of interest while they are camping.

Camping and backyard toys can be a hit on a camping trip. A kids' magnifying glass can be used to identify plants, insects, minerals in rocks, and flowers. Play games like I Spy, try bird-watching, look for animal tracks, or simply count rocks at the campground. A plastic bucket and shovel are ideal for digging in the dirt or playing in a shallow stream. While a few toys can help, know that simply exploring nature—and getting a little dirty—can be endlessly entertaining.

When it gets dark, kids love having their own flashlight, lantern, or headlamp. Make your sleeping space in the tent extra cozy, and consider bringing along a portable white-noise machine or a darkening tent cover to make sleeping in a bit easier.

There are other ways to involve the kids. Talk about what kind of food to bring, and let them help plan the menu. Knowing they can anticipate (and help with) some special campsite foods can make the experience more fun. For older kids and teens, consider letting them sleep in their own small tent. Some kids might like to invite a friend or enjoy their own private space.

Overall, strive to create a positive experience for your children—and yourself. Things won't ever go exactly according to plan, but showing kids how to be in nature, handle the unexpected, and have fun anyway is a wonderful life lesson.

CAMPING WITH DOGS

Dogs can be great camping companions. Use these basic guidelines when taking your four-legged friends into the wild.

- **LEASH YOUR DOG** to keep it from chasing wildlife and other campers and to protect it from getting lost and possibly attacked by wild animals. This can prevent you from cutting your trip short for an emergency vet visit.

- **ALWAYS PACK WATER FOR YOUR DOG,** and keep it from drinking out of streams and other natural water sources. Harmful bacteria, such as giardia, are a threat to dogs as well as humans.

- **MAKE SURE ALL YOUR DOG'S VACCINATIONS AND MEDICATIONS ARE CURRENT,** including rabies, *Bordetella*, and heartworm. If you're planning to camp in an area with Lyme disease, ask your vet about preventive measures.

- **AFTER CAMPING, CAREFULLY CHECK YOUR DOG FOR TICKS AND BURRS.** Prepare for accidents, and keep antibiotic cream and self-sticking bandage tape in your first aid kit.

- **KEEP YOUR DOG WARM.** Temperatures can drop quickly at night, so pack a dog vest, a puffy coat, or an extra blanket. Dog booties can protect tender paws and keep feet warm. Of course, plan to make space for your dog in the tent. Many dogs love to snuggle!

- **IT'S ESSENTIAL TO PACK OUT DOG POOP RATHER THAN LEAVE IT AT THE CAMPSITE.** Dog waste is not the same as that of other animals, even that of coyotes or wolves. It's dangerous to the environment, especially near water sources, and it makes a bad impression on the campers who use the site after you.

EASTERN COLORADO

Lakeside Campground at Jackson Lake State Park (see page 14)

1

⛺ Jackson Lake State Park Campground

Beauty: ★★★ / Privacy: ★★★ / Spaciousness: ★★★★ / Quiet: ★★★ / Security: ★★★★★ /
Cleanliness: ★★★★

Enjoy shoreline camping at this eastern plains oasis.

If you've never been to Jackson Lake State Park before, here's your chance. This beachy, starry-skied oasis has been ranked one of the top 15 park beaches by Reserve America, and in 2020, it was named an International Dark Sky Park, the first Colorado state park to earn the coveted designation.

A large warm-water reservoir, Jackson Lake is an important feature of the northeastern Colorado high-plains landscape. Local farmers depend on its water to irrigate their lands. But before these waters end up in the fields, they provide scenic recreational opportunities to all who know to come this way. The Rocky Mountains will always be a draw, but this Eastern Colorado state park is worth a look too. Campers can stay overnight in a slew of shoreline campsites while boating, sailing, swimming, and fishing on the 2,500-acre lake. A walk-in tent camping area and lakeside beaches make it even more appealing.

View from the tent-only campsites in Lakeside Campground at Jackson Lake State Park

KEY INFORMATION

LOCATION: Orchard

INFORMATION: Colorado Parks & Wildlife, 970-645-2551, cpw.state.co.us

OPEN: Year-round

SITES: 251

EACH SITE HAS: Picnic table, fire ring

WHEELCHAIR ACCESS: Site 35 only. All shower buildings have accessible stalls.

ASSIGNMENT: Reserve up to 6 months in advance.

REGISTRATION: cpwshop.com

AMENITIES: Hot showers, flush and vault toilets, laundry facilities, phone, electricity, marina

PARKING: At campsites or walk-in tent-campers parking area

FEE: $9 Parks Pass, plus $28–$36 per night (fees vary by site)

ELEVATION: 4,440'

RESTRICTIONS:

PETS: Must be leashed

QUIET HOURS: 10 p.m.–6 a.m.

FIRES: In fire grates only

ALCOHOL: None listed

VEHICLES: None listed

OTHER: 14-day stay limit in a 30-day period. Camping permits expire at noon. Limit of 2 tents and 6 people per site.

Several campgrounds border the west shore. The Lakeside Campground has wide-open, sun-whipped campsites farther from the lake, but nearer to the water, cottonwoods shade the preferred lakeside sites. A camper services building and shadier campsites lie closer to the lake. A set of walk-in tent sites stretches along the shoreline; these are the best sites in the park for tent campers. Sites 50 and 49 are closest to the shore. Don't forget your camping hammock, as each site has permanent posts for hanging a hammock and swaying by the water's edge. A swimming beach is near these walk-in tent sites.

The Cove Campground is more open. It has electrical hookups and caters more to RVs. The campsite picnic tables are protected by permanent shade structures. There is access to the swim beach here as well. The neighboring Pelican Campground offers four tent-only campsites a slight distance from the shore, near a pond. A foot trail connects the marina to the visitor center and also intersects with the Prairie Wetlands Nature Trail. Many of the other campsites here are more exposed to the elements. Boaters will want to take advantage of the quick access to the Shoreline Marina and boat ramp just north of the Pelican Campground.

The next campground, Sandpiper, lies on an open slope with numerous planted trees. The height of the hill allows for a great view of the lake but at the expense of shade and privacy. A camper services building and electrical hookups are located here.

Fox Hills is on a wide slope that offers views of the prairie and lake, which is fairly distant. The final campground on the west shore, Northview, is on an open slope under the sun's harsh rays. RVers may seek out this campground for its electrical hookups.

There is one more campground, Dunes, on the south shore of Jackson Lake. This small campground sits near some wooded dunes that separate you from the lake, but the water is just a short climb over the dunes. The campground has picnic shelters, and Russian olive and cottonwood trees provide shade. These are popular sites, and the small size of this campground makes for a quiet camping experience.

Water sports dominate the activities at Jackson Lake. Many visitors enjoy riding Jet Skis, power boating, and water-skiing during summer months. The Shoreline Marina, now under new ownership, sells limited fishing supplies and firewood but hopes to have paddleboard and kayak rentals in the future. The west and south shores are designated as wakeless areas, with two lakeside beaches where swimmers can cool off in the water and sunbathers can soak up some rays on the sand.

Bank fishing is popular in the Dike Fishing Area, where boats are prohibited. Both warm- and cold-water species inhabit the reservoir. Anglers drop lines for trout, walleye, wiper, perch, and crappie from the Dike Fishing Area and by boat throughout the lake. Ice fishing is also gaining popularity in the winter.

As for land activities, bicycling on the park roads is a popular choice. Campers can enjoy interpretive programs on summer weekends at the Cove Campground amphitheater. You can learn about Jackson Lake's wildlife, especially the wealth of waterfowl. And don't forget to peek out of your tent at the night sky, as the lake provides a natural mirror for the Milky Way above. Whether you explore by land or water, you will come away from this pride of the prairie with a new perspective on Colorado.

Jackson Lake State Park Campground

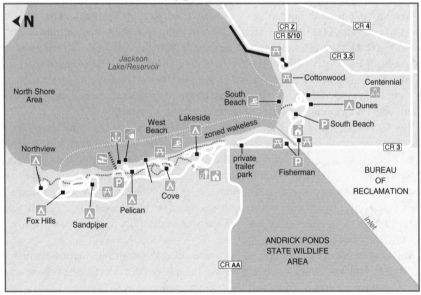

GETTING THERE

From Fort Morgan, head west on I-76 for 14 miles to Exit 66 and CO 39. Head north on CO 39 and follow it for 7.3 miles to CR Y5. Turn left on CR Y5 and follow it 2.5 miles to Jackson Lake State Park.

GPS COORDINATES: N40° 22.835'   W104° 05.400'

2

John Martin Reservoir State Wildlife Area: Lake Hasty and The Point Campgrounds

Beauty: ★★★★ / Privacy: ★★★ / Spaciousness: ★★★★ / Quiet: ★★★ / Security: ★★★★ / Cleanliness: ★★★★

Explore southeastern Colorado and enjoy vast lake vistas.

John Martin Reservoir State Wildlife Area, located 17 miles east of Las Animas, features one of the largest reservoirs in Colorado. Many consider the park a bird-watcher's paradise. More than 400 species have been documented in the area, including majestic bald eagles that roost here in the winter. Two species of federally protected shorebirds, the piping plover and the least tern, make their home in the park for several months each year.

This remote camping experience will keep you busy with activities. This is especially true if you've never ventured into southeastern Colorado or the Lower Arkansas River

Sami Colvin/Colorado Parks & Wildlife

View of the dam from The Point Overlook at John Martin Reservoir State Wildlife Area

KEY INFORMATION

LOCATION: Hasty

INFORMATION: 719-829-1801,
cpw.state.co.us

OPEN: Year-round

SITES: 213 (51 open in winter)

EACH SITE HAS: Picnic table, fire ring,
electrical hookups

WHEELCHAIR ACCESS: Sites 59 and 60 are
wheelchair accessible. An accessible fishing
pier and picnic area are available.

ASSIGNMENT: By reservation only

REGISTRATION: 719-829-1801,
cpwshop.com

AMENITIES: Hot showers, flush and vault
toilets, laundry facilities, phone, electricity,
swimming beach, playground

PARKING: At campsite

FEE: $9 Parks Pass, plus $17–$28 per night
depending on campground and season

ELEVATION: 3,851'

RESTRICTIONS:

PETS: Must be leashed

QUIET HOURS: 10:30 p.m.–6 a.m.

FIRES: In fire grates only

ALCOHOL: Permitted

VEHICLES: 1 vehicle per campsite unless
space permits

OTHER: 14-day stay limit in a 45-day period

Valley. The park service refers to John Martin as a "sapphire on the plains . . . a peaceful paradise." The reservoir provides undercrowded recreation: boating, riding Jet Skis, fishing, and more. The mild southeastern weather provides for many sunny days all year long.

The dam that created John Martin Reservoir was built in the early 1940s as an irrigation and flood-control project. Colorado State Parks took over management of the Lake Hasty area below the dam, the surface of the reservoir, and a portion of the north shore in October 2001 through a lease agreement with the U.S. Army Corps of Engineers.

A total of 213 campsites in this area accommodate everything from RVs to trailers to tents. There are plenty of RV sites here, but there are enough tent sites to keep you away from the large groups. The Lake Hasty Campground is located below the dam and provides plenty of shade thanks to a canopy of mature trees. The 109 campsites have electrical hookups and modern facilities, including centrally located water hydrants, coin-operated showers, laundry facilities, and flush toilets. In winter, sites 1–75 remain open, while sites 76–97 are closed from November 1 to March 15 to allow bald eagles to roost, hunt, and rest (one comfort station remains open during this time).

At Lake Hasty, sites 30–38 sit the closest to the shore. If you want to stay shore-bound, your best bet is to snag one of these spots that can accommodate vehicles up to 75 feet. Sites 10, 11, 13, 15, 18, 20, 22, 24, and 26 are 57-foot-plus electrical spots at the base of the dam and offer the privacy of an outside loop. All other sites are in a busy village of inside loops and turns within the campground. Not exactly tent camping, but not bad.

The Lake Hasty area has parking spaces and campsites that are accessible for people of all abilities. Sites 59 and 60 are ADA-accessible, 40-foot electrical camping spots close to the comfort station, showers, and laundry facilities. An accessible fishing pier and picnic area are available on the west shoreline of the lake. Restrooms, showers, picnic tables, drinking fountains, and grills accommodate everyone.

John Martin Reservoir State Wildlife Area: Lake Hasty Campground

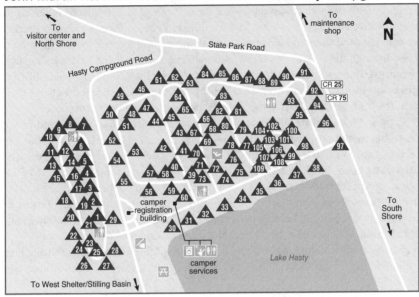

John Martin Reservoir State Wildlife Area: The Point Campground

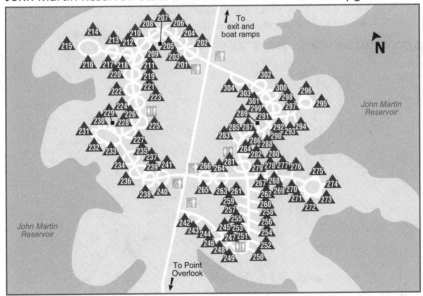

continued on next page

The Point Campground is located on the north shore and sits on a ridge overlooking John Martin Reservoir. There is no electricity, water, or shade, but there's plenty of incredible scenery. This campground is our choice for tent camping. Petroglyphs in the area suggest that Native Americans camped and lived here. Zebulon Pike, Kit Carson, and many other explorers and Colorado pioneers found their way into the valley. Traders and settlers traveled through the area while on the mountain route of the Santa Fe Trail. Remnants of the historic trail remain on the north shore of the park. The 4.5-mile Red Shin hiking trail begins below the dam and circles the Lake Hasty area through prairie and wetland environments. The trail then proceeds to the Santa Fe Historic Site on the north shore.

Fishing and water sports dominate recreation at John Martin Reservoir. Hand-propelled craft, sailboats, and boats with electric motors are permitted on Lake Hasty. John Martin Reservoir is open to all types of boating. The designated swimming area is at the swim beach at Lake Hasty below the dam. Fishing is permitted, with a valid fishing license, anywhere in the park, except from the boat docks and all areas closed to public access. The most common species caught at John Martin include walleye, saugeye, bass, crappie, muskie, wiper, catfish, perch, and bluegill. Lake Hasty is stocked in spring and fall with rainbow trout and cutthroat trout, which can be fished from the shore around the lake.

For true primitive camping elsewhere in the state wildlife area, purchase a valid hunting or fishing license, or a state wildlife area (SWA) pass, which gives access to all state wildlife areas, for $9 per day.

GETTING THERE

From Las Animas, take CO 50 east for 17 miles to Hasty. From Hasty, head south on CR 24 for 2 miles. The park visitor center will be on the right.

GPS COORDINATES: N38° 04.483' W102° 55.833'

3

⚠ Pawnee National Grassland: Crow Valley Family Campground

Beauty: ★★★★ / Privacy: ★★★★ / Spaciousness: ★★★ / Quiet: ★★★★ / Security: ★★★ / Cleanliness: ★★★

Head east for a high-plains pioneer experience.

If the Colorado mountains are what make the state famous, then the Colorado prairies are their lesser-known better half. Tent campgrounds are extremely limited east of I-25, the main interstate on the Colorado Front Range. That said, head in the direction of Pawnee National Grassland and the Crow Valley Recreation Area. With its uninterrupted vistas and its heritage, northeastern Colorado comprises an open book of nature with its own distinct and fragile beauty. Less populated and less trampled by tourists, this area is prime for discovery.

You can access this campground by traveling a portion of the Pawnee Pioneer Trail Scenic and Historic Byway. As you go, imagine how this shortgrass prairie was viewed by Native Americans, early cattle ranchers, homesteaders, and those who faced the Dust Bowl and Great Depression of the 1930s. After the failure of many farms during this last time frame, the US government purchased land from bankrupt farmers and instituted methods to restore land and vegetation that had been damaged by years of drought, plowing, wind, and water, thus creating the Pawnee National Grassland. Today, the national grassland covers almost 200,000 acres mixed with private land and is an internationally known birding area. Hiking, camping, picnicking, mountain biking, and sight-seeing are also popular recreational activities.

Site 9 at Crow Valley Family Campground in Pawnee National Grassland

KEY INFORMATION

LOCATION: Briggsdale

INFORMATION: U.S. Forest Service, Pawnee National Grassland; 970-346-5000; tinyurl.com/pawneenatgrass

OPEN: April–November

SITES: 10

EACH SITE HAS: Picnic table, fire pit

WHEELCHAIR ACCESS: Campsite 5 has a raised platform for easy access from wheelchair to tent, but all sites are wheelchair accessible.

ASSIGNMENT: Sites 1, 2, 3, 4, and 9 are reservable at recreation.gov; sites 5, 6, 7, 8, and 10 are first come, first served.

REGISTRATION: On-site

AMENITIES: Water, vault toilets, farm museum

PARKING: At campsite

FEE: $14 per day for a single unit, $20 per day for a double unit (plus reservation fee). Reservations are from 2 p.m. on day one to 2 p.m. the last day of your stay.

ELEVATION: 4,856'

RESTRICTIONS:

PETS: On leash

QUIET HOURS: None

FIRES: In designated fire pits

ALCOHOL: None listed

VEHICLES: 35'

OTHER: 14-day stay limit. Single units hold 5 people; double units hold 10 people.

Crow Valley Family Campground is just past the entrance to the Crow Valley Recreation Area, which is only a quarter mile off County Road 77. When you enter, pass by group picnicking and camping sites and the turnoff for the education site. The campground sits along Crow Creek, and the entrance is right next to the Birdwalk Trailhead. A grove of elm and cottonwood trees provides a unique respite in an otherwise open prairie.

There are 10 individual sites, laid out counterclockwise around a perfect circle. All campsites meet ADA requirements for accessibility. (There are also two accessible trails in the campground.) One double unit is available for those with special needs, and the rangers ask that you leave this unit open until all other spaces are filled. Sites 1, 2, and 3 are single campsites on the outer edge of the circle. Following them are sites 4, 5, and 6, which are the three double campsites. Sites 7, 8, 9, and 10 are closer to Crow Creek and sit on the western edge of the circle. Site 9 is the only site in the middle of the circle.

May and early June might be the best time to visit because the bird migration is in full swing, wildflowers are in bloom, and it is much cooler than the blazing months of July and August. Even during the cooler months, finding a shady campsite among the 10 is paramount. Large cottonwood trees shade the sites that ring the outer fringe of the campground. From these sites, short trails lead through the Crow Valley cottonwood groves and river thickets that attract birds and birders in large numbers. Not only are July and August hot, but the mosquitoes also swarm during this time. If you come during these hot months, be prepared.

Pawnee National Grassland offers hiking opportunities directly from the campground and within the prairie. The Pawnee Buttes are 30 miles northeast of the Crow Valley Recreation Area. The Buttes rise 300 feet above the surrounding prairie and are the result of the erosion of uplifted sedimentary beds deposited by ancient seas. The trail is open year-round and is an easy 1.5-mile hike to the base of the western Pawnee Butte. If you really want seclusion, dispersed camping is permitted anywhere on the grassland.

Pawnee National Grassland supports many bird species, especially during migration. The Colorado state bird, the lark bunting, is very common in the prairie in the spring and summer. Look for the pamphlet describing a self-guided motor-vehicle bird tour of the west side of the grassland, or pick up a brochure titled "Birding on the Pawnee by Automobile or Mountain Bike," perfect for mountain bikers. The history of the area is represented by many cemeteries, small museums, and preserved homesteads. Artifacts, arrowheads, fossils, and antique barnwood are easy to spot, but you must leave these items untouched.

Keep this campground at the top of your flatland list. It is an eye-opening experience to witness the magic of Colorado from the solitude of its open spaces. The mountain views are much different here than anywhere else in the state, with distant views of the snow-capped peaks. Large, fluffy clouds turn into dark thunderheads in a snap, which can create quite a show. This, along with the promise of fewer crowds and more quietude, should seal the deal.

Pawnee National Grassland: Crow Valley Family Campground

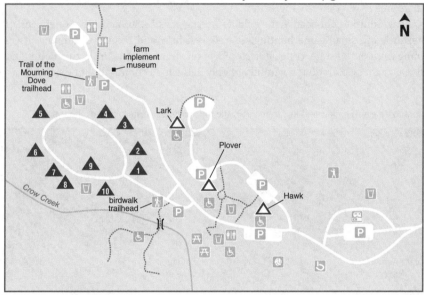

GETTING THERE

From the intersection of I-25 and CO 14, take CO 14 east 37 miles to Weld County Road 77. Take CR 77 a quarter mile to the campground.

GPS COORDINATES: N40° 38.750' W104° 20.233'

4

⚠ South Republican State Wildlife Area Dispersed Camping

Beauty: ★★★ / Privacy: ★★★★ / Spaciousness: ★★★★ / Quiet: ★★★★ / Security: ★★ / Cleanliness: ★★★

Your primitive prairie getaway in northeastern Colorado

South Republican State Wildlife Area is the easternmost camping area in this guidebook, and the most primitive. Located in a wide valley of the South Fork of the Republican River near the Kansas border, the wildlife area encompasses a former 1,900-acre reservoir originally built by the U.S. Bureau of Reclamation in the 1950s. The State of Colorado transformed the lake and the area around it into a state park (Bonny Lake State Park) in the 1970s, but in 2011, the lake was partially drained, and the land was converted into a state wildlife area (SWA) shortly thereafter.

Today, South Republican State Wildlife Area, spans 18,365 acres that offer deer, turkey, waterfowl, and small game hunting, as well as fishing and primitive camping. If you are coming from out of state, consider a stop here on your way to or from the mountains. You will realize that Colorado is beautiful not only in the high country but in the prairie as well.

Colorado's eastern prairie sees less traffic than the mountainous western part of the state.

Duane Stegner/Colorado Parks & Wildlife

KEY INFORMATION

LOCATION: Burlington

INFORMATION: Colorado Parks & Wildlife, 719-227-5200, cpw.state.co.us/swa

OPEN: Year-round

SITES: Dispersed

EACH SITE HAS: Primitive sites have no facilities. Most sites at North Cove Campground have picnic tables, fire rings, and shade shelters, and there's one vault toilet. Hale Ponds Campground has vault toilets.

WHEELCHAIR ACCESS: No designated accessible sites

ASSIGNMENT: First come, first served

REGISTRATION: Not needed

AMENITIES: Vault toilets, picnic tables, and shade shelters

PARKING: At designated parking areas off county roads

FEE: None, but a valid hunting or fishing license, or a state wildlife area pass ($9 daily) is required.

ELEVATION: 3,700'

RESTRICTIONS:

PETS: Must be leashed

QUIET HOURS: None

FIRES: In fire grates only

ALCOHOL: Permitted

VEHICLES: Designated roads only

OTHER: 14-day stay limit in 45-day period. Obey Colorado Parks & Wildlife rules and regulations; be aware of hunters in season; respect private property.

This surprisingly scenic slice of the prairie doesn't see the same crowds you might find in the mountains in the western part of the state. Generally, most of the visitor services, including the visitor center itself, have been closed for years. The good news is that there is plenty of primitive camping available—perfect for tent campers. After all, where there's no water and no electricity, there are also fewer RVs. Take note that there's also no cell service, so be sure to come prepared with what you need, and let someone know your plans and schedule in case of emergency.

You can also pitch a tent at any of the original, largely unmaintained campgrounds, like Foster Grove, Hale Ponds, North Cove, or Wagon Wheel. Be sure to park in designated parking areas and stay on the maintained roads. The current area-management staff provides maintenance services for North Cove Campground, a small cluster of sites on a simple dirt cul-de-sac near the old reservoir dam road. To get there, turn north on KK road, and then take a left after about 3 miles onto JJ road. This road takes you south toward North Cove Campground, which will be on your left.

Hale Ponds Campground is much more popular. This dispersed-camping area features a stretch of land along three large prairie ponds strung together in the shape of a horseshoe. This campground is kept in good condition, with vault toilets on either end and a maintained road throughout. It's especially nice for families, and the ponds are stocked with bass, bluegill, and trout—ideal for kids learning to drop a line.

Bonny Lake used to be a reservoir, but now it's essentially a low river. In the summer, irrigation systems draw on the aquifer, which drains it completely.

Wildlife viewing is a year-round pastime in South Republican State Wildlife Area, and there is more wildlife here than at many other plains reservoirs and river bottoms. You might see deer, raccoons, and opossums. Birdlife is particularly abundant, with golden eagles, bald eagles, red-tailed hawks, ducks, and all types of songbirds. Hunting is allowed in season.

For camping, consider spring or fall as prime time; summer brings temperatures over 100°F, and rainstorms can dump 6 inches in an hour. Check the forecast and be prepared. No matter what time of year you visit, you may be pleasantly surprised with what this old, new, growing, and transitioning area has to offer.

South Republican State Wildlife Area Dispersed Camping

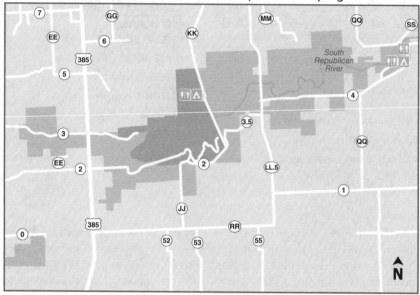

GETTING THERE

From I-70 in Burlington, drive north on US 385 for 21 miles. Turn right on CR 2 and follow it 1.5 miles into the South Republication State Wildlife Area.

GPS COORDINATES: N39° 36.513' W102° 11.267'

NORTH
CENTRAL
COLORADO

Aspenglen Campground (see page 71)

5

⛺ Buffalo Campground

Beauty: ★★★★ / Privacy: ★★ / Spaciousness: ★★★★★ / Quiet: ★★★ / Security: ★★★★ / Cleanliness: ★★★

A quick getaway for metro Denver–area mountain bikers, hikers, and families.

So many of the best national-forest campgrounds are high in the Rockies, where the weather and roads can be rough. But not Buffalo Campground. At 7,400 feet, it is high enough to escape the heat of the lowlands but not so high that you'll be dressing for winter in July. Buffalo Campground is near a network of trails, including the Colorado Trail, that wind through the ponderosa pines and strange rock formations that burst forth from the needle-carpeted forest floor. The best part? It's only 70 miles from the metropolitan Denver area.

The campground is situated in a stand of mature ponderosa pines on a gentle slope. Flowers, grasses, and juniper ground cover spread over the open, parklike forest floor. An ideal mix of sun and shade makes its way through the evergreens onto the very large camp-sites. Even the largest of tents will have no problem fitting on the level areas. However, the openness limits privacy.

After passing the fee station, you'll begin climbing up the hillside and pass an inner loop that splits off to your left; this loop has seven campsites that are more open than most because they border a small clearing in the center of the main loop. Most of the campsites are on the outside of the main loop and extend far back from the road. The higher you are on the loop, the better you can see a stone outcrop across the way where rock climbers go to work. Sites 12 and 17 are tent-only.

Buffalo Campground has large, level tent pads.

KEY INFORMATION

LOCATION: Bailey

INFORMATION: U.S. Forest Service,
Pike National Forest; 303-275-5610;
tinyurl.com/buffalocampgroundco

OPEN: Mid-May–late September

SITES: 38 (24 reservable; 14 first come,
first served)

EACH SITE HAS: Picnic table, fire ring,
tent pad

WHEELCHAIR ACCESS: Accessible sites,
picnic tables, and vault toilets are available.

ASSIGNMENT: By reservation or first come,
first served

REGISTRATION: 877-444-6777,
recreation.gov

AMENITIES: No water; vault toilets

PARKING: At campsites only

FEE: $27 per night (2 vehicles or 1 RV
per site); $6 for a third vehicle

ELEVATION: 7,400'

RESTRICTIONS:

PETS: Must be leashed

QUIET HOURS: 10 p.m.–6 a.m.

FIRES: In fire rings only

ALCOHOL: At campsites only

VEHICLES: 1 site can accommodate a 40'
vehicle; others have max lengths of 15'–32'

OTHER: 14-day stay limit

A campground host is stationed on the loop, usually at site 2, to quell any late-night parties or direct you to the many recreational opportunities in the area. There are vault toilets but no water.

Plan to reserve a site here to ensure you get a spot. Weekends usually see a mix of families and youthful, active folks, the vast majority of whom are tent campers. It's quieter during the week. No matter when you come, there is plenty to enjoy in the surrounding Pike National Forest.

As mentioned, rock climbers scale the formation across from the campground. Mountain bikers are seen everywhere, riding the trails that wind through the Buffalo Recreation Area and beyond. A favorite ride is the Colorado Trail. Keep going up the hill from the campground and you will intersect the trail. You can turn left out of the campground on the Colorado Trail and bike to CO 126, then return via Forest Service Road (FS) 550. Trail 722 makes a loop off the Colorado Trail south. Just off FS 550 is another loop that heads toward Miller Gulch. Make up your own loop in the trails that twist and turn amid the pines and pillars of stone.

Access Buffalo Creek across from the campground entrance. This creek offers trout fishing and a nice place to dip your toes in the water. Find more mountain biking along FS 543.

Hikers can enjoy the same trails as the mountain bikers. You can also head into the Lost Creek Wilderness, just a few miles northwest of Buffalo. From the trailhead off Wellington Lake Road, hikers can take the Colorado Trail into the wilderness high country or walk the Craig Meadows Trail into Craig Creek. Other hikes into this wilderness are also accessible from this trailhead.

If you'd like a little lakeside diversion, head over to Wellington Lake. This private lake is just a short drive away, with day-use areas for swimming, fishing, boating, and stand-up paddleboarding. Wellington Lake also offers excellent camping right on the water or along the surrounding hillsides, with a variety of hikes for all levels.

In the summer, there's still enough light to make the drive from Denver or Colorado Springs and be sitting at Buffalo Campground at dusk by the campfire, where you can cook up a good supper and retire to your tent before jumping onto your favorite trail by morning.

Buffalo Campground

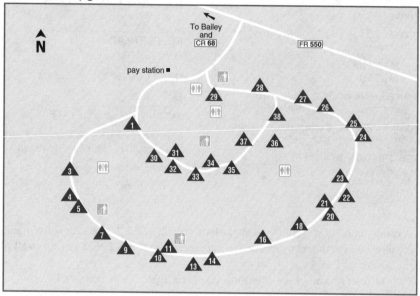

GETTING THERE

From US 285 in Bailey, head southeast on County Road 68 (it turns into FS 543) for 7 miles. Turn left on FS 860/FS 550/Redskin Creek Road and follow it 4 miles to Buffalo (sometimes called Buffalo Creek) Campground, which will be on your right.

GPS COORDINATES: N39° 20.548' W105° 20.138'

6

The Crags Campground

Beauty: ★★★ / Privacy: ★★★★ / Spaciousness: ★★★ / Quiet: ★★★★ / Security: ★★★ / Cleanliness: ★★★★

Colorado State Forest is rich in wildlife and is one of the state's best places to see moose.

The Crags is an appropriate name for this campground, which is balanced on the steep slopes of the Never Summer Mountains in State Forest State Park. The treeless, granite precipices are not far above you and your vista of Diamond Peaks. The namesake Nokhu Crags are behind the campground, out of sight. The camping season is short, and nights are always cool here. So reserve a few nights in July or August and prepare for a special experience.

This area abuts Rocky Mountain National Park, which gives you an idea of the level of scenery here. North Park, the vast expanse of meadowland in Jackson County, is known as the moose capital of Colorado. Plan to see a few of these huge creatures and more animals on the trails—and potentially even at your campsite. When I camped here, a very confident moose caused quite the stir by getting a taste of a fellow camper's breakfast cereal one morning. Keep an eye out and keep your distance.

Sunset over The Crags Campground in State Forest State Park

KEY INFORMATION

LOCATION: Walden

INFORMATION: Colorado Parks & Wildlife, 970-723-8366, tinyurl.com/thecragsco

OPEN: Year-round

SITES: 25

EACH SITE HAS: Picnic table, fire grate, tent pad

WHEELCHAIR ACCESS: ADA fishing access

ASSIGNMENT: By reservation only

REGISTRATION: 970-723-8366, cpwshop.com

AMENITIES: Vault toilets, water

PARKING: At campsites only

FEE: $28 per night, plus $9 Parks Pass

ELEVATION: 10,000'

RESTRICTIONS:

PETS: Must be leashed

QUIET HOURS: 10 p.m.–6 a.m.

FIRES: In fire grates only

ALCOHOL: Permitted

VEHICLES: No trailers or motor homes allowed

OTHER: 14-day stay limit in 45-day period

After driving the dizzying last mile to The Crags, take a deep breath and enter the campground. The setting is a high-country forest of subalpine fir and Engelmann spruce growing densely on steep slopes. The campsites have been leveled, though you may have to go up or down a bit to reach the camp from your car.

Don't drive too fast through the loop or you'll miss some of the campsites, which are set back in the woods. A few sites have pull-through areas for your vehicle, but don't expect to see any big rigs up here. The road in discourages them (as do the rangers), but any passenger car smaller than a movers truck can make the drive.

Enter a sunny area where you will see tree stumps left over from the days when this area was logged. Campsites here have a clear view of the severe lands above them. The loop reenters the woods, and the more heavily wooded campsites begin. The last three sites are very isolated and offer the most solitude. Back at the beginning of the loop are vault toilets, one of which was recently redone; the hand-pump well is to your left in the woods a bit. Be prepared; the water here is ice-cold.

Weekdays rarely find the campground filled. However, on later summer weekends this hidden jewel of a park will be alive with campers, though not nearly as busy as other Front Range parks.

The Crags is close to some of the best hiking in the 71,000-acre Colorado State Forest. Just up the road is the trail to Lake Agnes, well worth a visit while you're here. It's less than a mile from the trailhead to the lake, which is banked against the Nokhu Crags. A path makes a loop around the lake, which is banked against the Nokhu Crags. A path makes a loop around the lake. Hike 4.1 miles from the American Lakes Trailhead to Snow Lake, with views of the Medicine Bow Mountains. Make the one-way walk to Cameron Pass and have a shuttle car pick you up. You might see mountain lions, elk, mule deer, coyotes, and bears, so stay on high alert. Check out the visitor center, with its eye-catching barbed-wire moose outside and informative displays on the park's wildlife.

Ruby Jewel Lake, Kelly Lake, and Clear Lake are other destination hikes in the park. If you fish these waters, remember that only artificial lures and flies are allowed. State regulations apply in park streams and in North Michigan Reservoir and the Ranger Lakes.

A bit more on the moose: In 1995, the Colorado Senate declared North Park the moose capital of Colorado. Moose were introduced into North Park in the late 1970s and have been thriving here ever since. Try to observe moose in the early morning and late evening in the willow thickets along area creeks. You could also take the auto tour of the Arapaho National Wildlife Refuge in the heart of North Park. Get directions at the visitor center. Be sure to respect the wildlife, and always give moose plenty of space.

The Crags Campground

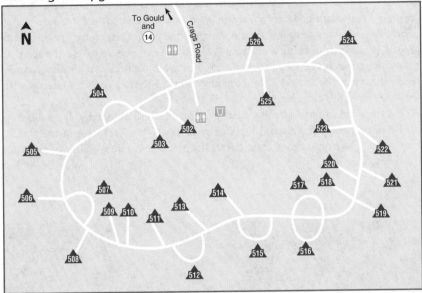

GETTING THERE

From Gould, drive north on CO 14 for 7 miles to Forest Service Road (FS) 170. There will be a sign for Lake Agnes. Turn right on FS 170 and follow it 0.5 mile to the first intersection. Turn right on FS 172 and climb steeply 1 mile, turning left at the next intersection. Continue to The Crags Campground.

GPS COORDINATES: N40° 30.155' W105° 53.407'

⛺ Elbert Creek Campground

Beauty: ★★★★ / Privacy: ★★★ / Spaciousness: ★★★★★ / Quiet: ★★★ / Security: ★★★ / Cleanliness: ★★★

You can walk from your tent and hike up Mount Elbert, Colorado's highest peak at 14,433 feet.

Note: This campground was closed indefinitely due to road work at press time, but I chose to keep it because of its popularity. Some of this information may be outdated once it reopens.

Elbert Creek has an agreeable location, high in the mountains along a resonant stream, where you get a sense of being away from it all. Active campers stay here, though it seems that they are not around enough to really take in the atmosphere of the campground. Hiking is the main exercise; trails to Mount Elbert and the Mount Massive Wilderness are just a short walk from the campground.

There are also lakes and streams nearby for fishing, and mountain bikers like to pedal up to Mount Champion Mill and the Colorado Trail—the backbone of the state's trail system. Somehow, campers find time to eat, sleep, and rest a little before going at it again the next day.

Mount Elbert, the tallest peak in Colorado

Tampa/Shutterstock

KEY INFORMATION

LOCATION: Leadville

INFORMATION: U.S. Forest Service, Pike–San Isabel National Forests, Cimarron and Comanche National Grasslands, Leadville Ranger District; 719-486-0749, tinyurl.com/elbertcreekcg

OPEN: June–September

SITES: 17

EACH SITE HAS: Picnic table, fire grate

WHEELCHAIR ACCESS: No designated accessible sites

ASSIGNMENT: First come, first served; no reservations

REGISTRATION: Self-registration on-site

AMENITIES: Pump well, vault toilets, trash collection

PARKING: At campsites only

FEE: $20 per night (2 vehicles or 1 RV per site); $7 for a third vehicle

ELEVATION: 10,000'

RESTRICTIONS:

PETS: Must be leashed

QUIET HOURS: 10 p.m.–6 a.m.

FIRES: In fire grates only

ALCOHOL: None listed

VEHICLES: 16'

OTHER: 14-day stay limit

The small campground is laid out underneath a lodgepole pine forest in a flat along Halfmoon Creek. As you enter the campground, the road splits into two drives running parallel to Halfmoon Creek. Vehicle turnarounds at the end of each drive provide room for more streamside campsites. The forest is virtually devoid of ground cover, save for a few small saplings and rocks. However, the brush thickens alongside Halfmoon Creek, which flows loud and clear below the campground.

The right-hand drive has nine campsites, and the left-hand drive has eight campsites; avoid the last three campsites on this side unless you want to see who is driving by.

The pump well and vault toilets are conveniently located between the two drives. Because Elbert Creek receives heavy use from hikers, try to get there on Friday night or early Saturday if you are a weekend warrior. Otherwise, look for a spot at the nearby Halfmoon East Campground and Halfmoon West Campground.

Hikers love to bag peaks here in the Centennial State, and the highest point in Colorado, Mount Elbert, is very close. Elbert is the second-highest point in the lower 48 states, behind Mount Whitney in California. It is a 3.5-mile climb to the crest from the nearby trailhead. There's nothing technical about this well-marked and maintained trail, though snow may present a problem even in the early summer. You can also make a loop hike from here using the North Mount Elbert, South Mount Elbert, and Colorado Trails.

Just a short walk up the road is the Mount Massive Wilderness. Much of this wilderness is above treeline, so bring adequate clothing for inclement weather. Mount Massive is the second-highest peak in Colorado, only 12 feet lower than Mount Elbert, so you can stay at Elbert Creek Campground and climb the two highest peaks in the state. Just beyond the Mount Elbert Trailhead, take the Colorado Trail north into the wilderness up to the Mount Massive Trail, and hike to the peak. You can also climb the North Halfmoon Lakes Trail, which starts a couple of miles up Forest Service Road (FS) 110. Farther up this road is the Champion Mine, with its aerial tramway still intact. You can bike or drive to the Champion Mine.

The Iron Mike Mine site is a hike or bike up South Halfmoon Creek. Nearby Emerald Lake features a picnic area and offers fishing, as do all the previously mentioned creeks. Speaking of fish, you might check out the Leadville National Fish Hatchery. Established in 1889, it is the second-oldest federal fish hatchery in the country. Fish from here have been placed all over the Rockies, and today it still produces brook, cutthroat trout, and rainbow trout. There are trails on the hatchery grounds as well, with great views of the big mountains you came here to climb.

Elbert Creek Campground

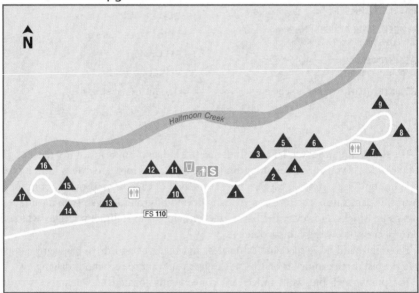

GETTING THERE

From Leadville, head south on US 24 for 4 miles to County Road (CR) 110 and the sign for the Leadville National Fish Hatchery. Turn right here and follow CR 110 for 0.7 mile to Halfmoon Creek Road. Turn left on Halfmoon Creek Road and follow it a short ways before the sharp right turn to stay on Halfmoon Creek Road. Continue on Halfmoon Creek Road as it turns into FS 110. Elbert Creek Campground will be 4 miles up on your right.

GPS COORDINATES: N39° 09.128' W106° 24.815'

8

Pinewood Reservoir Campground

Beauty: ★★★★ / Privacy: ★★★ / Spaciousness: ★★★★ / Quiet: ★★★ / Security: ★★★★ /
Cleanliness: ★★★★

Great camping east of Rocky Mountain National Park and one of the best tent camping options between Loveland and Estes Park

Many of the millions of tourists who arrive in Rocky Mountain National Park do so via Loveland. Tent campsites between Loveland and Estes Park are few and far between; however, Larimer County offers a few gems that are easy to get to from US 34, the main highway leading to the park. Because these campgrounds are tidy and the scenery is beautiful, Larimer County is a nice place to stay whether or not you're on your way to Rocky Mountain National Park.

While the other Larimer County open spaces in this area also provide camping access, Pinewood Reservoir outshines them for those who prefer tent camping. The campground is approximately 10 minutes west of Loveland and about 40 minutes east of Estes Park. The drive up Big Thompson Canyon Road is a long crawl, especially during the summer months when campers are practically bumper to bumper up the winding road. If you can, time your visit in the early fall; not only will it cut your drive time, but you might also be able to use the campground as a base camp for exploring Rocky Mountain National Park.

Campsite overlooking Pinewood Reservoir

KEY INFORMATION

LOCATION: Loveland

INFORMATION: Larimer County Natural Resources, 970-679-4570, larimer.org/naturalresources/parks/pinewood-reservoir

OPEN: Year-round

SITES: 27

EACH SITE HAS: Fire grate, picnic table

WHEELCHAIR ACCESS: Sites 3, 4, and 27 are ADA-accessible.

ASSIGNMENT: By reservation only

REGISTRATION: 800-397-7795, larimercamping.com

AMENITIES: Vault toilets, water, day-use parking, picnicking, natural play area

PARKING: At sites or walk-in tent-campers parking area

FEE: $20–$55 per night depending on season and site; $10 daily entrance permit

ELEVATION: 6,580'

RESTRICTIONS:

PETS: Must be leashed

QUIET HOURS: 10 p.m.–6 a.m.

FIRES: In fire grates only

ALCOHOL: Only at campsites

VEHICLES: 30'

OTHER: Capacity varies by site; maximum 8 people in largest sites; no boating; 14-day stay limit; stay 100' away from dam.

This campground is adjacent to Larimer County Parks and Open Lands' Carter Lake, Flatiron Lake, and Ramsay-Shockey Open Space. The landscape here is semiarid, with brush, small trees, red rock, and bluffs.

Pinewood Campground lies along Pinewood Reservoir, a 100-acre reservoir surrounded by 327 acres of public lands. No boats with motors are allowed on Pinewood Reservoir. Only hand-launched craft like kayaks, stand-up paddleboards, and inner tubes are allowed on the water in this area, making it an ideal getaway for a little mountain fun without driving too far from the Front Range. Be warned, though: Pinewood Reservoir is accessible only by a narrow 4-mile paved road with very steep 8%–10% grades. That, plus the modest size of the campsites, means that big motor homes and RVs tend to stay away and camp at nearby Carter Lake instead.

The entire campground has been recently remodeled. You'll encounter the 15 standard electric sites here first. These have the best lake access, although the smaller RVs that do make it up the road tend to pick these spots. Instead, I recommend reserving one of the 12 walk-in tent campsites. Drive past the day-use area and past site 16 to the walk-in tent camping parking spots on the left. These are higher up on a steep slope but offer more privacy and beautiful views from behind a natural screen of trees. These sites are best for solo campers or couples, as they are too steep for young children and too small for groups.

Many folks come to Pinewood Campground to fish, relax, or just picnic for the day. The Bison Visitor Center is close to the campground and has plenty of information on the area. If you feel like getting cleaned up and spending money, an outlet shopping center and a new lifestyle mall sit on the far eastern edge of Loveland near I-25.

If you really want a change of pace, there are many areas along this Colorado Front Range corridor and into Wyoming that are accessible from Pinewood. From Loveland, go north to Fort Collins (30-minute drive) and enjoy the college town vibe or regional recreational opportunities. Horsetooth Reservoir, Lory State Park, and Poudre Canyon are honorable mentions. If you go south, you can visit Boulder (30-minute drive) or Denver (1-hour drive). Or go even farther north into Wyoming (1-hour drive) and open up a whole new world of Western fun.

Pinewood Reservoir Campground

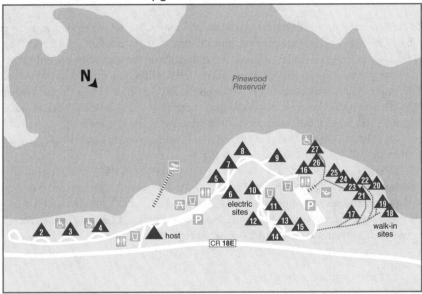

GETTING THERE

From Loveland, drive west about 7 miles on US 34 to turn left on County Road (CR) 29 (also known as Carter Lake Road). In 2 miles, turn right onto CR 18E, travel 6.6 miles, and end at Pinewood Reservoir.

GPS COORDINATES: N40° 21.831' W105° 16.944'

9

Gold Park Campground

Beauty: ★★★★★ / Privacy: ★★★ / Spaciousness: ★★★★★ / Quiet: ★★★★ / Security: ★★★★ /
Cleanliness: ★★★★

At the end of the rainbow is a place like Gold Park.

Gold Park is nearly the ideal tent campground. It is somewhat out of the way, on a dirt road, small, well kept, in a picturesque setting, and adjacent to many outdoor attractions. The dirt road leads up Homestake Valley, a scenic watershed in the Sawatch Range. Gold Park, with only 11 campsites, is located along Homestake Creek, which is hemmed in by Homestake and Whitney Peaks. These mountains are protected as part of the Holy Cross Wilderness. This wilderness area, like most, offers the best recreation of the national forests, mountain biking excepted. Several trailheads are a short drive away. The historic mining town of Holy Cross City is only a 4-mile walk or a rugged four-wheel-drive trip away. Homestake Reservoir and Homestake Creek offer decent fishing.

Gold Park is set in a wooded flat between Homestake Creek and a low-lying hill covered in trees and boulders. Beyond the pay station the drive veers right, passing the campground host. Lodgepole pines and other smaller conifers shade the entire campground. Large, spacious camping areas are spread along the loop as you proceed up the gravel drive, which then veers left as the rocky hill launches toward Homestake Creek.

A campsite by the creek at Gold Park Campground

KEY INFORMATION

LOCATION: Minturn

INFORMATION: U.S. Forest Service, White River National Forest; 970-827-5715; tinyurl.com/goldparkcg

OPEN: Late May–late September

SITES: 11

EACH SITE HAS: Picnic table, fire grate

WHEELCHAIR ACCESS: No designated accessible sites

ASSIGNMENT: First come, first served; no reservations

REGISTRATION: Self-registration on-site

AMENITIES: Vault toilet, trash collection; no water

PARKING: At campsites only

FEE: $21 per night

ELEVATION: 9,300'

RESTRICTIONS:

PETS: Must be leashed

QUIET HOURS: None

FIRES: In fire grates only

ALCOHOL: At campsites only

VEHICLES: 40'

OTHER: 10-day stay limit

The campsites come closer to the road as the vehicle turnaround approaches. Three of the best sites are here, one snug against a shaded rock outcrop and the other two lying next to Homestake Creek. These last two sites are the biggest and most coveted sites at Gold Park.

A single vault toilet serves this quaint camping area. Gold Park receives moderate use, filling up on the usual holidays. About the only RV you will see here is the campground host's. It is unusual, but good, to have a host in a campground this small. The mood here is serene, with the creek providing a naturally symphonic backdrop and muffling some of the ATV noise along Homestake Reservoir Road.

The upper part of this valley was once home to the mining town of Holy Cross City. The first mines were staked in 1880; Gold Park Mining Company was formed in 1881. The ore assays promised a boom. However, the outer layer of ore proved to be the richest, and the gold wasn't nearly as rich at deeper levels. By 1884, it was finally admitted that the mine was a bust. Another attempt was made in the same area in 1896; a deep tunnel was dug, but the profit just wasn't there. You can take Forest Service Road (FS) 759 up to the site of this mine by foot, bike, or jeep. These days, your only strikes will be from fish on Homestake Creek or Homestake Reservoir, 3 miles up FS 703, your route to Gold Park; the 480-acre lake is brimming with trout.

Take time to explore the Holy Cross Wilderness, including the area's alpine lakes and icy streams. The Fall Creek Trail starts about 2 miles up the road to Holy Cross City. The trail heads up to Hunky Dory Lake and the stair-stepping Seven Sisters Lakes, where rock cliffs make for watery backdrops.

You can also try Missouri Lakes Trail, a 1,500-foot climb over 3 miles. The trail starts up FS 704 and goes above the timberline. A shorter walk to a high-country lake is the Fancy Pass Trail, which also starts off FS 704 above Gold Park. It's a mere 2 miles to Fancy Lake, which has spectacular scenery and perfect shoreline seats for dipping sore feet. Treasure Vault Lake is another mile beyond, though you have to go over Fancy Pass and then down-hill to the lake.

Down from Gold Park is the Whitney Lake Trail, which offers views on its 2.3-mile journey to Whitney Lake. From here you can scale 13,271-foot Mount Whitney, rising on the north shore of the lake, if you follow the west ridge to the top. No matter where you go in the Holy Cross Wilderness, know that this place is a real gold mine in the Colorado outdoors.

Gold Park Campground

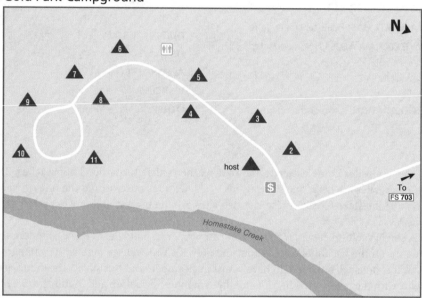

GETTING THERE

From I-70 near Minturn, head south on US 24 for 11.5 miles to FS 703 (Homestake Road). Turn right on FS 703 and follow it for 7 miles to Gold Park Campground, which will be on your left.

GPS COORDINATES: N39° 24.267' W106° 26.122'

⛺ Golden Gate Canyon State Park Campgrounds

Beauty: ★★★★ / Privacy: ★★★ / Spaciousness: ★★★ / Quiet: ★★★★ / Security: ★★★★★ /
Cleanliness: ★★★★

This tent camping getaway is only 30 miles from the Denver metropolitan area.

Golden Gate Canyon State Park is a preserved slice of the Rocky Mountains just a short drive from Denver. Rock spires stand out among rich forests and green meadows. Outstanding views of the Continental Divide extend toward the west. Well-marked and well-maintained trails meander down watery glens to open meadows where settlements once stood. This refuge is rich in wildlife, from birds to bears. With 55 walk-in tent sites, your camping experience promises to be a good one.

There are two primary campgrounds at Golden Gate Canyon. Reverend's Ridge is the big one; it offers spaces for every type of camper. There are 10 camp loops of every shape and description, including small circles with parking areas radiating like spokes. There are two loops with pull-through sites for RVs.

Tent campers need only concern themselves with loops F, G, and J in Reverend's Ridge; these offer walk-in tent sites. Loops F and G are next to each other. It's a short walk from the parking area to your tent site beneath lodgepole pines or an aspen grove or two. Loop J is at the very end of the main camping drive, cutting down on drive-by traffic. Some of the campsites are close to the parking area; others are set back in the woods. A stay at Reverend's Ridge offers tent campers a bonus: you can stay at the tent sites and still access the water spigots and the hot showers and flush toilets located in the camper services building.

Aspen Meadow is more rustic and the preferred area for tent campers. It has hand-pump wells and vault toilets and is more scenic and isolated from the rest of the campground. The area is broken up into four distinct walk-in tent camping areas.

The Meadow Loop has 14 campsites in a conifer and aspen wood, next to a large meadow. The sites on one side of the dirt road are situated amid large boulders that add to the character of the area. The Twin Creek and Conifer Loops are off the ridge in a small valley. The woods are denser here, and a small stream adds to the setting. These are the most popular

Large boulders add character to some sites at Golden Gate Park's Aspen Meadow Campground.

KEY INFORMATION

LOCATION: Golden

INFORMATION: Colorado State Parks, 303-582-3707 or 303-642-3856 (summer), tinyurl.com/ggcanyonsp

OPEN: Aspen Meadow: mid-May–mid-October; Reverend's Ridge: year-round but limited services outside of Memorial Day–Sept. 30

SITES: 132

EACH SITE HAS: Picnic table, fire grate

WHEELCHAIR ACCESS: ADA-accessible fishing pier at Kriley Pond. ADA-accessible tent sites 30HD and 72HD are reservable only by calling 800-244-5613.

ASSIGNMENT: By reservation only

REGISTRATION: 800-244-5613, cpwshop.com

AMENITIES: Hot showers, flush and vault toilets, laundry, phone, vending. Reverend's Ridge has 59 campsites with electrical hookups.

PARKING: At campsites or walk-in tent-campers parking area

FEE: $10 Parks Pass, plus $18–$36 per night

ELEVATION: 9,100'

RESTRICTIONS:

PETS: Must be leashed

QUIET HOURS: 10 p.m.–8 a.m.

FIRES: In fire grates only

ALCOHOL: None listed

VEHICLES: 40'

OTHER: 14-day stay limit in 45-day period

tent-only sites and are the first to be claimed. Some of the campsites are nearly 100 yards away from the parking area.

The Rimrock Loop has several wooded campsites up on a ridge punctuated with boulder landscaping; these sites offer a view of the lands in the distance. Vault toilets are located in each loop at Aspen Meadow.

For a more rugged experience, Golden Gate Canyon also offers four backcountry shelters and 20 hike-in backcountry tent sites. All of these are approximately 1–2 miles from the nearest parking spot. All sites have bear boxes, and tent sites share a double bear box located between sites. No fires are allowed, and reservations are still required.

No matter where you camp, reservations are mandatory, as with all Colorado State Parks. Reserve early to ensure you get the site you want. Weekdays are less of a problem in this safe, family-oriented campground and natural area.

While you are in the campground, check the notices about ranger programs that are held in Reverend's Ridge on weekend nights. These include kids programs on weekend days that cater specifically to young campers who want to have a good time and learn something about nature without feeling like they're in school.

Other campers will want to strike out on their own on some of the 35 miles of park trails, which are open year-round. Everyone should walk the Raccoon Trail. It begins at Panorama Point, where you have a fantastic view of the Continental Divide, and it has interpretive signs to teach hikers a thing or two. The most popular loop hike is the Mountain Lion Trail, which winds for 7 miles into Forgotten Valley, back up a canyon, and up by Windy Peak. Take the side trail to the top of Windy Peak.

The walk into Frazer Meadow is one of the more picturesque park settings. There are three ways to get to the meadow, including the Mule Deer Trail, which connects to Aspen Meadow Campground. There are five ponds in the park and a few small streams that offer trout fishing. Dude's Fishing Hole is very near Aspen Meadow. This quick getaway has so much to offer, ideal for city dwellers who need a taste of real, natural Colorado.

GETTING THERE

From Golden, take CO 93 north 1 mile to Golden Gate Canyon Road. Turn left and follow Golden Gate Canyon Road 15 miles to the park.

GPS COORDINATES: N39° 52.554' W105° 26.942' (Reverend's Ridge)
N39° 52.102' W105° 25.030' (Aspen Meadow)

Golden Gate Canyon State Park: Reverend's Ridge Campground

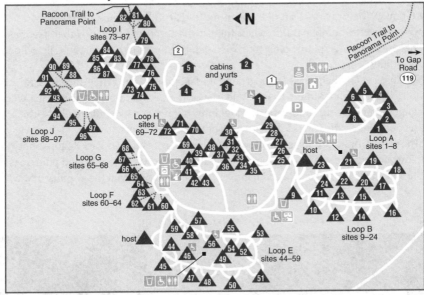

Golden Gate Canyon State Park: Aspen Meadow Campground

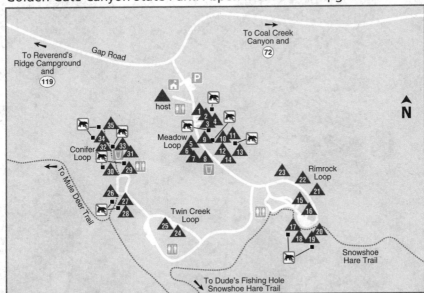

11

Guanella Pass Campground

Beauty: ★★★★ / Privacy: ★★ / Spaciousness: ★★★ / Quiet: ★★★ / Security: ★★★ / Cleanliness: ★★★

The Mount Evans Wilderness is just a hike away from Guanella Pass Campground.

Guanella Pass Campground is located steps away from one of Colorado's most scenic byways. Guanella Pass Road is a stretch of 22 miles between the towns of Georgetown and Grant. What was once an old wagon route that linked the two mining towns today draws bumper-to-bumper traffic when the aspens turn gold in September. Georgetown and neighboring Silverplume offer tourist-friendly glimpses into Colorado's silver-boom of the late 1800s.

Camping at Guanella Pass Campground is ideal for exploring the Arapaho & Roosevelt National Forests and Mount Evans Wilderness. It also offers prime access for wildlife-viewing, scenic driving, landscape photography, hiking, and even off-roading. The area is not recommended for RVs, so it's a great spot for tent campers.

The campground occupies two loops on either side of Guanella Pass Road/County Road 381. Throughout the campground are thick stands of spruce, fir, aspen, and pine trees providing some privacy and shade and dampening vehicle noise from the popular byway.

South Clear Creek near Guanella Pass Campground

KEY INFORMATION

LOCATION: Georgetown

INFORMATION: U.S. Forest Service, Arapaho & Roosevelt National Forests and Pawnee National Grassland, Clear Creek Ranger District; 801-226-3564; fs.usda.gov/arp

OPEN: June 3–Sept. 11

SITES: 17

EACH SITE HAS: Tent pad, picnic table, fire ring, charcoal grill

WHEELCHAIR ACCESS: No designated accessible sites

ASSIGNMENT: By reservation (5 sites are first come, first served)

REGISTRATION: 877-444-6777, recreation.gov

FACILITIES: Vault toilets, water spigots, trash dumpsters

PARKING: At campsites only

FEE: $23 per night

ELEVATION: 10,900'

RESTRICTIONS:

PETS: On leash only

QUIET HOURS: 10 p.m.–6 a.m.

FIRES: In fire rings only

ALCOHOL: At campsites only

VEHICLES: 45'

OTHER: 14-day stay limit

Turn west to access sites 1–6. These are the first-come, first-served campsites each with a tent pad, fire ring, picnic table, and charcoal grill. Some sites do allow for RV camping or trailers of varying lengths, but keep in mind there's no accessibility or electricity. Sites 2 and 3 are close together, and sites 5 and 6 are closest to the vault toilet.

Cross the road to the other loop and arrive at sites 8–18 (there is no site 7). Sites 9–15 are tent-only sites with gravel driveways. Sites 13–18 are clustered around an oval-shaped drive, and site 13 is closest to the vault toilet.

At this campground you have the Mount Evans Wilderness hiking experience in your backyard. It's only a 6-minute drive to the Bierstadt Trailhead, where you can start the long walk up one of Colorado's most-trekked fourteeners. Farther up County Road 62 is Guanella Pass at 11,669 feet—the easiest way to achieve higher elevation. Keep an eye out for mountain goats and bighorn sheep. Note that Guanella Pass Road is closed every year between Thanksgiving and Memorial Day.

You're also just down the road from Silver Dollar Lake Trailhead, a short hike to two scenic lakes. The altitude and occasional steep climbing may be challenging. Note that the trail leads to Naylor Lake first, which is on private property; enjoy the sights and sounds, but please do not trespass. The second lake, Silver Dollar Lake, is for public use. Trout fishing can be found on the South Fork of Clear Creek.

Farther south is the trailhead for Abyss Lake Trail. This trail climbs strenuously along the glacier-carved valley of Scott Gomer Creek for 7 miles to Abyss Lake. The lake lies perched in a cirque, an encircling wall of rock with Mount Bierstadt on one side and Mount Evans on the other.

Keep in mind that if you plan on recreating in the Mount Evans Wilderness, you will need to fill out a self-issued permit. These permits have no associated quotas or fees and are in place to help manage visitation. Find them at each trailhead. Simply fill out the permit and drop the stub into the register box.

Because this area is so popular, there are heavy restrictions on when and where you can camp. If you can't get a reservation and the first-come, first-served sites are full, try Burning Bear Campground, located right next to the Abyss Trailhead. For dispersed camping, head to Forest Service Road 119. Drive 1 mile past the Geneva Park Campground (currently closed for the foreseeable future) and look for signs for parking and camping. There are approximately 30 designated dispersed campsites along the road for first-come, first-served use.

Guanella Pass Campground

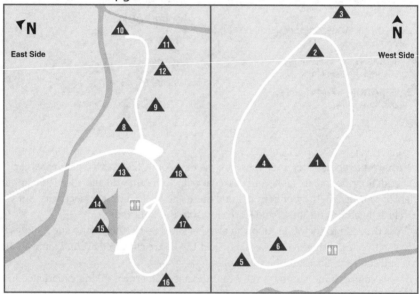

GETTING THERE

From Georgetown, go south on CR 381 (Guanella Pass Scenic Byway) for 9 miles.

GPS COORDINATES: N39° 36.767' W105° 42.967'

12

Hermit Park Open Space: Hermit's Hollow Campground

Beauty: ★★★★ / Privacy: ★★★★ / Spaciousness: ★★★★ / Quiet: ★★★★ / Security: ★★★★ / Cleanliness: ★★★★

The historic Hermit Park Open Space is a haven near Estes Park and Rocky Mountain National Park.

Hermit's Hollow campground is located in Larimer County's Hermit Park Open Space. Hermit Park opened in 2008 approximately 2 miles southeast of Estes Park. One of the highlights of this campground is Kruger Rock Trail, which offers a rarely seen perspective of Rocky Mountain National Park. The views alone are worth the trip.

The campground is just one aspect of the tidy area that was once a retreat for a private corporation. Before that, Hermit Park was a cattle ranch. Legend has it that a loner named Dutch Louie built a cabin on this land in 1910 and squatted here under an arrangement with the ranchers. Apparently, parents would warn their children to "stay out of the hermit's park!" The name stuck.

Plentiful ponderosa pines ensure that Hermit's Hollow Campground stays alive with green in winter.

KEY INFORMATION

LOCATION: Estes Park

INFORMATION: Larimer County Natural Resources, 970-577-2090, larimer.org/naturalresources/parks/hermit-park

OPEN: March 1–Dec. 20

SITES: 42

EACH SITE HAS: Fire grate, picnic table

WHEELCHAIR ACCESS: Sites H10 and H21 are designated ADA-accessible.

ASSIGNMENT: By reservation only

REGISTRATION: 800-397-7795, larimercamping.com

AMENITIES: Comfort station, dump station, picnic shelter and tables, ranger station, drinking water

PARKING: At sites or additional parking area

FEE: $35–$65 per night depending on site, plus $10 daily entrance permit. Entrance permits are available at gatehouses and self-serve stations prior to entering the parks, or online. Campers who pre-purchase permits can bypass the entrance gates and proceed directly to their campsite upon arrival.

ELEVATION: 7,880'

RESTRICTIONS:

PETS: Must be leashed

QUIET HOURS: 10 p.m.–6 a.m.

FIRES: In fire grates only

ALCOHOL: None listed

VEHICLES: 40'

OTHER: 2-night stay required for weekends; 3-night stay required for holidays

Today, it's a fine place for a camping getaway. Hermit Park Open Space is nestled in hills dotted with wildflowers in the summer and always alive with green amid the plentiful ponderosa pine trees. The starting elevation here is 7,880 feet with an elevation gain on the Kruger Rock hike of more than 1,000 feet, topping out the park at 8,964 feet. The cabins are rustic but charming, and the tent campsites are top-notch. RV sites are thrown in for good measure. The entire place is laid out for maximum enjoyment of this beautiful piece of mountain real estate.

Hermit's Hollow is the first of a network of five campgrounds. It has 42 non-electric campsites. After that is a cabin loop with 13 rustic cabins available for rent. Bobcat Campground comes next with 39 non-electric campsites; Kruger Campground has 5 equestrian campsites, and Granite Gulch Campground is a group camping area with 5 sites. Any campsite here is a winner, but I especially liked Hermit's Hollow. No generators are allowed, and there are three lovely walk-in tent camping sites.

Many people come to Hermit Park Open Space from the Front Range to relax or hike. Visitors also use the open space as a jumping-off point for Estes Park and the fun of Rocky Mountain National Park. The town of Estes Park is approximately 2 miles northwest of Hermit Park. The Kruger Rock Trail offers unique views of Longs Peak, the Estes Valley, and the Continental Divide. The Homestead Meadows Connector Trail is an easy trail for hikers, mountain bikers, and horseback riders to access Homestead Meadows. This 1-mile trail goes to the U.S. Forest Service boundary and 12 miles of trails.

A group pavilion is unique to the Hermit Park Open Space. A 40-acre picnic area with a covered pavilion, volleyball court, horseshoe pits, and picnic tables accommodates up to 250 people. Many in the area use the site for special events, such as weddings, family reunions, and company picnics.

Hermit Park Open Space

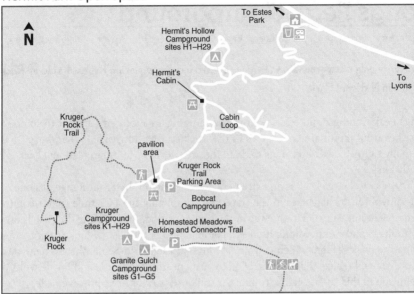

GETTING THERE

From Denver, take I-25 north to CO 66 and travel west on CO 66 for 16 miles to Lyons. Turn right onto West Main Street onto CO 36 West. Continue on CO 36 for 16.7 miles. The entrance to Hermit Park is on the left.

GPS COORDINATES: N40° 21.367' W105° 27.416'

13

⛺ Rocky Mountain National Park: Longs Peak Campground

Beauty: ★★★ / Privacy: ★★ / Spaciousness: ★★★ / Quiet: ★★ / Security: ★★★★ / Cleanliness: ★★★★

This tent-only campground can be your base camp for exploring the east side of Rocky Mountain National Park.

Longs Peak Campground offers a tent-only camping area located adjacent to some of the most beautiful mountain landscapes in the Rockies. The downside is that, because there are many sights to see and things to do in the area, Rocky Mountain National Park is constantly busy.

The hike to Longs Peak is an extremely popular one on the Front Range. It's one of the best-known fourteener hikes in the state, and completing the 14.5-mile round-trip trek is a badge of honor. Starting in the wee hours each morning, cars will line the road leading to the trailhead and campground. It takes a combination of timing and luck to get a campsite during the peak season, which is from late June through mid-September. When you snag a spot, you will realize that in spite of all the cars nearby, the hustle and bustle won't overwhelm you in this 26-site campground; the trailhead parking area, however, will.

Longs Peak as seen from the Keyhole Route

Steve Boice/Shutterstock

LOCATION: Estes Park

INFORMATION: National Park Service, 970-586-1206, nps.gov/romo

OPEN: Year-round

SITES: 26

EACH SITE HAS: Picnic table, fire grate, tent pad

WHEELCHAIR ACCESS: No designated accessible sites

ASSIGNMENT: First come, first served; no reservations

REGISTRATION: Self-registration on-site

AMENITIES: Water, vault toilets (no water October–May); seasonal trash collection

PARKING: At campsites only

FEE: $35 per night (Memorial Day–mid-September, plus $25 park entrance fee.

ELEVATION: 9,400'

RESTRICTIONS:

PETS: Must be leashed; not allowed on trails

QUIET HOURS: 10 p.m.–6 a.m.

FIRES: In fire grates only; gathering of firewood prohibited

ALCOHOL: At campsites only

VEHICLES: No RVs

OTHER: 7 nights per campsite June–September; 14-night limit in winter; maximum of 8 people per site

Pass the line of parked cars along Longs Peak Road and come to a split in the road. Turn right and enter the campground. To your left is the always-full-in-summer trailhead parking. The teardrop-shaped, gravel campground loop makes its way beneath a lodgepole woodland pocked with boulders and smaller trees. The sites are mostly on the outside of the loop and have somewhat-obstructed views of the Twin Sisters peaks across the Tahosa Valley in the Roosevelt National Forest.

More campsites are stretched along the peak side of the loop. As popular as they are, they are well maintained. A hill rises against the campground. This is the campground's rockier side; campsites are more spread out over here. Overall, the sites are average in size, with ample room for the average tent. But always being full does result in a little less peace and a little more . . . pizzazz. Still, it helps to know you're probably all camping here for the same reason.

Water spigots are situated around the campground, but there are only two toilets, one for men and one for women, located in the center of the campground. You might have to wait in line for that, too. Despite the crowds, people generally still have a pleasurable tent camping experience here. Try to visit during the shoulder seasons—June or late September. Bring your own water and a warm sleeping bag if you come in winter.

If you have some time, and especially if you're adjusting to the altitude, spend a day doing some shorter hikes or scenic drives through Estes Park or Rocky Mountain National Park. Driving Trail Ridge Road is a must; it's a rite of passage at Rocky Mountain National Park. The views are as exhilarating as the air is cold up there. Then check out the exhibits and self-guided nature trail at Moraine Park Museum. Back at Longs Peak, take a warm-up hike on the Storm Pass Trail. It leads up to the Eugenia Mine Site and on to Storm Pass after 2.5 miles.

Go to bed as early as possible and tackle Longs Peak the next morning. The park service recommends that you try to leave the trailhead between 3 a.m. and 6 a.m. to make the

7-plus miles to the summit by noon. Your route to the top of Longs Peak will be the Keyhole Route, which is generally free of snow from mid-July until mid-September. Bad weather can arise at any time but is more likely in the afternoon during the summer. Bring plenty of warm clothes and lung power. The final part of the route is 1.6 miles past the end of the maintained trail. This is considered a high-risk hike, so be prepared with supplies and water. The round-trip lasts 11–15 hours. Be sure to keep your campsite a second night because you will be too exhausted to do anything except make supper and hit the sack.

Just a few miles south of Longs Peak is the Wild Basin area, a quieter section of the park's east side. Many old-time Rocky Mountain enthusiasts consider this to be the best area of the park. Many watery features in the basin make great day hikes. It is only 0.3 mile from the ranger station in Wild Basin to Copeland Falls. Calypso Cascades is 1.8 miles up, where Saint Vrain Creek splits. Ouzel Falls is 2.7 miles up the trail from the ranger station. Continue a little farther to see the peaks above and the plains below. There are several alpine lakes to access in Wild Basin.

Rocky Mountain National Park: Longs Peak Campground

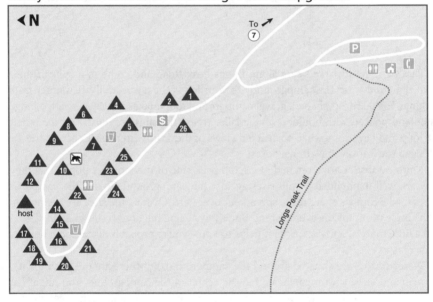

GETTING THERE

From Estes Park, head south on CO 7 for 8 miles to Longs Peak Road. Turn right on Longs Peak Road and follow it 3 miles to Longs Peak Campground, which will be on your right.

GPS COORDINATES: N40° 16.471' W105° 33.462'

14

Lost Park Campground

Beauty: ★★★★ / Privacy: ★★★★ / Spaciousness: ★★★★ / Quiet: ★★★★ / Security: ★★★ /
Cleanliness: ★★★

Lost Park is your camping ticket to the Lost Creek Wilderness.

Lost Park Campground sits atop a knoll in the large valley at the confluence of Indian Creek, North Fork Lost Creek, and South Fork Lost Creek. The Kenosha and Tarryall Mountains serve as your campground cathedrals. It is in this enhanced setting that you can set up your tent, then fish, hike, and explore the Lost Creek Wilderness until the call of civilization is too loud to ignore.

You won't want to leave this small, hilltop campground cloaked in lodgepole pines and complemented by other conifers. With only 12 campsites and nearly 20 miles of dirt road, civilization doesn't exactly come knocking on your tent flap. Two drives with vehicle turnarounds at their ends divide the campsites, which are spread very far apart. There is one set of vault toilets on each loop.

The first drive circles the top of the knoll. Most of the campsites are on the more heavily wooded left side, while the few on the right look over Lost Creek below and Bison Peak above. Campsite 10 lies in the rocky center of the auto turnaround. Other boulders serve as parking spot barriers.

Michael Petrarca/Rocky Mountain Recreation Company

Surrounding landscape near Lost Park Campground

KEY INFORMATION

LOCATION: Fairplay

INFORMATION: U.S. Forest Service, Pike–San Isabel National Forests, Cimarron and Comanche National Grasslands; 719-836-2031; tinyurl.com/lostparkcg

OPEN: May–September

SITES: 12

EACH SITE HAS: Picnic table, fire grate

WHEELCHAIR ACCESS: No designated accessible sites

ASSIGNMENT: First come, first served; no reservations

REGISTRATION: Self-registration on-site

AMENITIES: Hand-pump well, vault toilets, picnic tables, fire rings

PARKING: At campsites only

FEE: $15 per night

ELEVATION: 10,000'

RESTRICTIONS:

PETS: Must be leashed

QUIET HOURS: 10 p.m.–6 a.m.

FIRES: In fire grates only

ALCOHOL: At campsites only

VEHICLES: 22'

OTHER: 14-day stay limit

The lower drive turns left and drops toward the North Fork of Lost Creek. Two campsites lie on a slope to your left. Stay here if you don't mind sleeping a little tilted. Pass the northbound section of the Brookside-McCurdy Trail. Follow the drive as it swings right along the creek, passing the well pump in a meadow. The next three campsites offer excellent privacy and spaciousness on a small hill looking downstream on Lost Creek; these sites also feature a mix of lodgepole pines and other conifers. Then you come to the vehicle turnaround with one more large campsite on your right.

The campground manager told me that multiple improvements will be coming in 2022, but regardless of amenities, the three fishable streams and three trailheads at the campground will make you appreciate Lost Park more than anything else. The Lost Creek Wilderness, which is most of the land you see around you, is almost 120,000 acres of meadows, woods, and unusual granite formations, where one of Colorado's largest herds of bighorn sheep lives. There are nearly 100 miles of trails to enjoy, and you can probably get most of the hiking you desire without restarting your vehicle until it's time to head home.

The Wigwam Trail heads east along Lost Creek proper. Soon you'll come to the very large East Lost Park. This is a huge meadow that goes on and on. Veer right on an unmaintained fishing trail if you want to keep going down Lost Creek. The Wigwam Trail follows a feeder stream up and over a divide to the Wigwam Creek drainage.

The north end of the Brookside-McCurdy Trail skirts the wilderness; mountain bikers can pedal this section. It then intersects the Colorado Trail, where you can either veer right into the wilderness high country or veer left and keep on biking to the top, over to the Craig Creek drainage. If you go south on the Brookside-McCurdy Trail from the campground, you will head up Indian Creek toward Bison Pass. There are fishable waters with small but spunky trout ready to tear at your lure on all the creeks.

Mountain bikers can't enter the wilderness, but they have their own trails to use just back down Forest Service Road (FS) 56. Walleye Gulch Road (FS 854) and Topaz Road (FS 446) can be used with other connecting Forest Service roads to make loops. I recommend the Colorado Trail Explorer (COTREX) app for getting comprehensive information about Colorado's trail systems free on your device, downloadable ahead of time. Get all your supplies before you get anywhere near the area; Lost Park is far from the main roads. The nearby towns are small and don't have much in the way of supplies except for the convenience store variety. If you have room to pack them, bring your binoculars to help you spot bighorn sheep.

Lost Park Campground

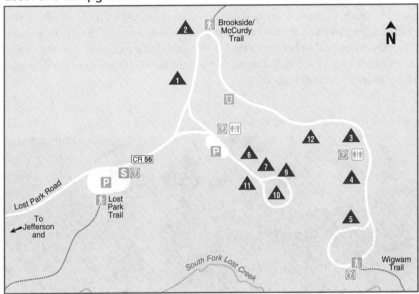

GETTING THERE

From Jefferson, drive north 1 mile to County Road (CR) 56 (Lost Park Road), turn right, and drive east 19 miles to the dead-end at Lost Park Campground.

GPS COORDINATES: N39° 17.067' W105° 30.367'

15

The Narrows Campgrounds: Lower

Beauty: ★★★ / Privacy: ★★★ / Spaciousness: ★★ / Quiet: ★★★ / Security: ★★★★ / Cleanliness: ★★★★★

The Lower Narrows, right on a wild river, is the best tent camping in the canyon.

The Poudre (pronounced pooh-der) River is full of plenty of river lore and conjures up images of French trappers hooting down fierce rapids in the canyon. Its official name is *Cache la Poudre* River, and legend has it that the river was named when a party of westward fur trappers was forced to lighten its load, which included gunpowder, near the banks after being caught in a heavy snowfall. The order was given to *cache la poudre* or "hide the powder" so that it could be retrieved the following spring.

Camp on the Cache La Poudre River at Lower Narrows Campground.

KEY INFORMATION

LOCATION: Livermore

INFORMATION: U.S. Forest Service, Arapaho & Roosevelt National Forests, Pawnee National Grassland; 970-295-6700; tinyurl.com/lowernarrowscg

OPEN: Mid-May–mid-September

SITES: 8

EACH SITE HAS: Fire grate, picnic table, tent pad

WHEELCHAIR ACCESS: No designated accessible sites

ASSIGNMENT: By reservation only

REGISTRATION: 877-444-6777, recreation.gov

AMENITIES: Vault toilets, bear lockers, water (usually available through late September)

PARKING: Lot for exactly 8 cars

FEE: $23

ELEVATION: 6,400'

RESTRICTIONS:

PETS: Must be leashed

QUIET HOURS: 10 p.m.–6 a.m.

FIRES: In fire grates only

ALCOHOL: Permitted

VEHICLES: Passenger vehicles only

OTHER: Limit of 8 people per site

The Poudre River, with its designation as a Wild and Scenic River, is quite wild. One area that is sacred is a section called the Narrows, a narrow cleft where the river has cut through the rock walls. Even driving through this area can be dicey, with hairpin turns, blind spots, and looming canyon walls. If you're driving through the canyon in springtime, park at a pulloff and watch the water crashing down, full of the cold, spring snow runoff. The Class VI rapids tear into the canyon walls and pummel anything in their path. (River rapids are rated on a difficulty scale starting at I, considered easy, and ending at VI, considered extremely difficult and dangerous.)

The Narrows Campgrounds, both Upper and Lower, are located just above said rapids. Poudre Canyon recreationists are usually limited to RV-clogged camping areas, with one exception. The Lower Narrows is the tent-only portion of the Narrows Campground, complete with a separate entrance, and is by far the best tent camping in the canyon. There is plenty of hiking, especially in the nearby Comanche Peak Wilderness. Anglers, off-road enthusiasts, and Sunday drivers all jam up the roadway, especially during the summer weekends, but all seem to be having a great time. The Poudre River is the main draw to the Narrows Campgrounds, and the Lower Narrows campsites are as close as you can get to sleeping onshore, especially preferred sites 12 and 13. Site 14 is a good second choice, and site 15 isn't bad either but is a little higher above the river. Light sleepers take note: the river rages through here in May and June with accompanying noise. All sites are walk-in tent sites, but you won't have far to walk for any of them.

Lower Narrows Campground is configured as a loop. At the entrance, take a right turn. Numbering starts at site 8 because Lower Narrows and Upper Narrows (sites 1–7) are managed jointly by the ranger district at the Narrows Campground. Park at the parking lot right next to site 8. There is an obvious disadvantage to being near the parking lot. Sites 8, 9, and 10 are closer to the road. Sites 11–15 are scattered about from here. As mentioned before, sites 12 and 13 are most popular, with 14 not far behind and 11 and 15 earning honorable mentions.

Even in other months this is not a sleepy stretch of river, but a rather steep and rocky section, as is most of Poudre Canyon. The river may be boated by experienced rafters and kayakers above this area and again resuming at Stevens Gulch, 2.5 miles downstream. Between the campground and Stevens Gulch are the several Class VI drops hidden from the road. Lower Narrows Campground is a good alternative to the high-use, RV-type campgrounds in the area. There are very few services for miles in either direction except for a few seasonal stores. If you are interested in rafting or kayaking, the Poudre River is open to both private and commercial boaters; I recommend setting up an outfitted trip in Fort Collins before heading out.

The Narrows Campgrounds

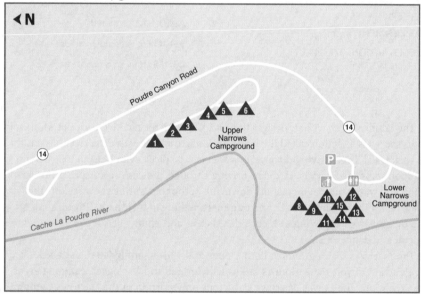

GETTING THERE

Drive 7 miles north of Fort Collins on US 287. Turn left on CO 14, also known as Poudre Canyon Highway, and drive approximately 16 miles west. If coming from upper Poudre Canyon/Cameron Pass, look for the entrance just after Narrows Campground.

GPS COORDINATES: N40° 41.353' W105° 25.950'

16

Peaceful Valley and Camp Dick Campgrounds

Beauty: ★★★★ / Privacy: ★★★ / Spaciousness: ★★★★ / Quiet: ★★★ / Security: ★★★★ /
Cleanliness: ★★★★

The access to Indian Peaks Wilderness and Rocky Mountain National Park is second to none at this camping area situated in a glacial valley adjacent to Middle Saint Vrain Creek.

Technically two campgrounds, Peaceful Valley and Camp Dick are connected by a short road and appear to be one and the same. Camp hosts buzz around in golf carts, keeping the area tidy. RVs are also in attendance, and summer-camp crowds are frequent. So why include this area in a tent camping book, you ask? With thoughtfully laid-out sites, a picturesque wooded landscape, and proximity to the creek, the wilderness, and the national park, it's a place where all campers seem to live in harmony. In fact, RV campers may convert to smaller accommodations after they see what amazing spots are available for tent campers.

Wide-open campsites at Camp Dick

KEY INFORMATION

LOCATION: Allenspark

INFORMATION: U.S. Forest Service, Arapaho & Roosevelt National Forests, Pawnee National Grassland; 303-541-2500; tinyurl.com/campdickcg and tinyurl.com/peacefulvalleycg

OPEN: Mid-May–mid-November

SITES: 58 (41 at Camp Dick; 17 at Peaceful Valley)

EACH SITE HAS: Picnic table, fire ring, upright grill, tent pad

WHEELCHAIR ACCESS: Camp Dick accessible sites: 7–10, 12, 29–38; Peaceful Valley accessible sites: 2–7, 9, and 15–17

ASSIGNMENT: First come, first served and by reservation

REGISTRATION: Camp Dick: Sites 1–5, 11, 13–20, 24, 26, 28, and 39–41 are first come, first served; sites 7-10, 12, 21-23, 25, 27, and 29–38 are reservable.

Peaceful Valley: Sites 8 and 10–17 are first come, first served; campsites 1–7 and 9 are reservable. Reservations can be made between Memorial Day and Labor Day weekends by calling 877-444-6777 or visiting recreation.gov.

AMENITIES: Water, vault toilets

PARKING: At campsite

FEE: $17.25–$46 per night

ELEVATION: 8,650'

RESTRICTIONS:

PETS: Must be leashed

QUIET HOURS: None

FIRES: In designated areas

ALCOHOL: Permitted

VEHICLES: 50'

OTHER: 14-day stay limit; maximum 8–12 people per site (varies by site)

Access to the Indian Peaks Wilderness and Rocky Mountain National Park is the reason to be here. You can start hiking directly from the Saint Vrain Trailhead at the west end of the campground. Backpackers, horseback riders, mountain bikers, OHV users, and anglers all enjoy the advantages of the surroundings. Since Indian Peaks is a wilderness area, those wanting to camp or recreate within the wilderness boundary should contact the Boulder Ranger District regarding specific regulations. The same goes for Rocky Mountain National Park, so contact the National Park Service for rules particular to that area. It's important to note that without entering the wilderness or national park, there is plenty to do. The campground itself is still in the national forests.

It's been a while since Peaceful Valley and Camp Dick have been remodeled, but the paved road and the regular upkeep make this campground feel updated and welcoming. Some sites at Peaceful Valley and Camp Dick are not recommended during peak season because of lack of privacy and the fact that they are essentially set up for RVs. But there are a few that are the cream of the crop, especially if you can get here during the week. Of the 58 campsites, here are the top 12. By far the best for privacy and space is Camp Dick site 35, at the end of a loop. Camp Dick sites 12, 21, 32, 38, 40, and 41 are also recommended for space and privacy. Sites 38 and 40 are double campsites. Peaceful Valley site 1 is the final pick because a slight embankment provides extra privacy, and it is also right on the edge of Middle Saint Vrain Creek. Although we've narrowed the choices, keep in mind that all of the campsites are scattered among spruce, pine, and aspen trees, and all have tent pads, parking, and fire areas.

Entering Peaceful Valley, you cross Middle Saint Vrain Creek to find site 7 directly to the left. A right turn takes you into a nice, small loop that starts with our favorite site, 1; circles counterclockwise to 2, 3, 4, 5, and 6; and then deposits you back to site 7. Site 8 is usually the host site; site 9 is on the right, next to the drinking water. Sites 10–14 are in a cluster on the left. Those are walk-in tent camping sites just a short walk from a parking area. These were some of my favorites. Sites 8–17 generally have denser trees and more shelter than sites 1–7.

Leave Peaceful Valley and enter Camp Dick. On the right are sites 1–9, which are quite close together and have few trees or little privacy. However, favorite sites 40 and 41, on the left, offer lots of privacy and beautiful scenery even though they're a bit close to the road. Continue toward the right and pass site 12, a favorite; 17 looked OK, but I would avoid sites 13, 18, and 19 as they looked too sunny and too close to the toilets for my liking. Sites 20, 21, 22, and 23 are on the right side of a new loop; sites 24, 26, and 28 are inside the loop and not recommended. Sites 26 and 27 are on the opposite side. Site 26 wasn't a favorite because it sits in the open, and site 27 is very close to the vault toilet. As the loop ends, a straightaway hosts 10 good choices. Site 35 is at the far end of all these sites—so far at the end of the turnaround loop, in fact, that it's our number-one pick.

This area was once the site of a Civilian Conservation Corps camp established in the 1930s. Now the campground is open to all. Mountain biking is allowed on the first 5 miles of Buchanan Pass Trail, so you can make a loop from Peaceful Valley or Camp Dick via Buchanan Pass Trail and Middle Saint Vrain Road. If you're into off-roading, the Middle Saint Vrain and Bunce School roads are popular. And for equestrians, guided horseback riding is available at Peaceful Valley Lodge, a mile away.

These campgrounds fill up by Friday afternoon in the summer, so plan to arrive early, consider making a reservation, and try to take time off during the week to really take advantage of this beautiful place.

Peaceful Valley Campground

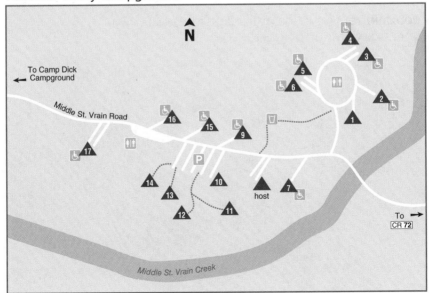

Camp Dick Campground

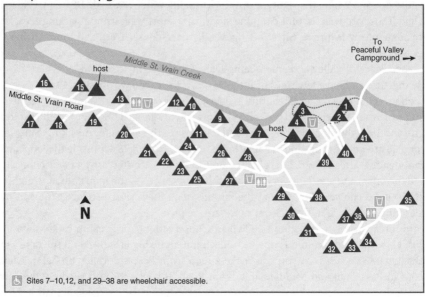

Sites 7–10,12, and 29–38 are wheelchair accessible.

GETTING THERE

Peaceful Valley Campground is off CO 72 (also known as the Peak to Peak Highway) at mile marker 50, approximately 19 miles north of Nederland and 20 miles south of Estes Park. It may also be accessed via CO 66 west to Lyons, then southwest on CO 7 for approximately 12 miles to CO 72, and south on CO 72 approximately 4 miles.

GPS COORDINATES: N40° 07.950' W105° 30.533' (Peaceful Valley)
  N40° 07.742' W105° 31.146' (Camp Dick)

Rainbow Lakes Campground

Beauty: ★★★★ / Privacy: ★★★ / Spaciousness: ★★★★ / Quiet: ★★★★ / Security: ★★★ / Cleanliness: ★★★

Rainbow Lakes is Boulder County's best high-country tent camping getaway.

The first thing you should know is that the last couple of miles to Rainbow Lakes are bone-jarringly bumpy. But once you get here, you'll wonder why you didn't come sooner. This is an old campground that still feels special. The picnic tables, grates, and grills are still in decent shape, and the campground host keeps the bathrooms nearly sparkling.

The campground is just south of Rocky Mountain National Park and adjacent to the equally scenic Indian Peaks Wilderness. The forest here is primarily lodgepole, with some Engelmann spruce and a few aspens struggling to survive. On my late-August visit, the aspens had barely started leafing out.

If you are in the area, this is where you should stay. The Rainbow Lakes are only half a mile from the campground. Make your visit up to the lakes for the day, and camp down at the campground. That preserves the natural resource and concentrates your impact at the campground. Rainbow Lakes Campground can also be a base camp for exploring the east

View from one of the walk-in campsites at Rainbow Lakes Campground

KEY INFORMATION

LOCATION: Nederland

INFORMATION: U.S. Forest Service, Boulder Ranger District; 303-541-2500; tinyurl.com/rainbowlakescg

OPEN: Mid-June–mid-September

SITES: 18

EACH SITE HAS: Picnic table, tent pad, fire grate, bear locker

WHEELCHAIR ACCESS: No designated accessible sites

ASSIGNMENT: First come, first served; no reservations

REGISTRATION: Self-registration on-site

AMENITIES: Vault toilets, trash services; no water

PARKING: At campsites only

FEE: $17 per night

ELEVATION: 10,000'

RESTRICTIONS:

PETS: Must be leashed

QUIET HOURS: 10 p.m.–6 a.m.

FIRES: In fire grates only

ALCOHOL: At campsites only

VEHICLES: 20'

OTHER: 14-day stay limit; maximum 8 people allowed per site

side of Rocky Mountain National Park. Be forewarned: this campground receives heavy weekend use in late summer, and there are signs posted everywhere to discourage dispersed camping along the road. Stated simply, come here during the week or Sunday night if at all possible for a quieter, more pleasant experience.

Rainbow Lakes Campground lies along a stream emanating from the Rainbow Lakes that feed into Caribou Creek. Drive past the Rainbow Lakes Trail and Arapaho Glacier Trail parking circle, and arrive at the campground. Make your first right, pass the host site and vault toilet, and then find parking for the walk-in, tent-only sites (15, 16, 17, and 18). As a solo female camper, this felt like a great setup: close enough to the toilet and near enough to the host if I had any questions, but a nice enough walk away in a spot that felt both private and spacious. In late august, the stairway to my site was lined in fuchsia fireweed.

The rest of the campsites continue along the road following the stream and are spread well apart beneath the trees. Sites 1, 2, 4, 6, and 9 are right on the creek and especially desirable. The last campsite, site 8, is a double site accommodating up to 15 people, logically set away from the others. This used to be the public trailhead for the Rainbow Lakes Trail, an easy 1-mile walk to the namesake lakes, but now hikers are directed to the trail via the Arapaho Glacier connector trail. This is great for us tent campers because it means fewer people tramping through the campground—although I did see and hear some hikers walking that trail through the trees above my site, so it's not a perfect solution.

Speaking of tramping through the campgrounds, be aware that you're in bear and moose country, and use the provided bear boxes. There are two clean vault toilets for this small campground, and one at the main trailhead.

From Nederland, you drove part of the Peak to Peak Scenic Byway. Continue to enjoy this drive north to Estes Park, where there are supplies, or south to Black Hawk and Central City, where there is legalized gambling. The casinos offer limited-stakes gaming.

However, a sure bet is the Indian Peaks Wilderness next door, home to the southernmost glaciers in North America. This high wilderness starts at 10,700 feet. Much of the scenery is austere tundra, rock, and ice. The Arapaho Glacier Trail runs in and out of the wilderness a few miles up to the Arapaho Glacier overlook. The glacier is on this side of North Arapaho Peak. It's 6 miles from the trailhead to the Arapaho Pass Trail. Other trailheads into the busy Indian Peaks lie to the north off forest roads that intersect the Peak to Peak Byway.

Another area to consider is the Wild Basin of Rocky Mountain National Park. This is a watery place, where many cascades tumble down from the heights and picturesque lakes lie beneath craggy peaks. The basin is north on the Peak to Peak Byway. Luckily, it was left unscathed by the 2020 wildfires that raged through parts of Rocky Mountain National Park. Get hiking information from the ranger station there.

Rainbow Lakes Campground

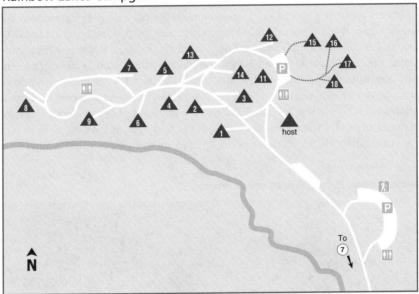

GETTING THERE

From Nederland, drive north on CO 72 for 6.5 miles to Forest Service Road (FS) 298 (also known as County Road 116). There will be a sign for University of Colorado Mountain Research Station. Turn left on FS 298 and follow it 6 miles to Rainbow Lakes Campground.

GPS COORDINATES: N40° 0.625' W105° 34.267'

18

Robbers Roost Campground

Beauty: ★★★★ / Privacy: ★★★ / Spaciousness: ★★★★ / Quiet: ★★★ / Security: ★★★ / Cleanliness: ★★★★

Steal away to this easy campground getaway.

Robbers Roost conjures up images of Wild West outlaws and hideouts for bandits who may have just had a shootout at the O.K. Corral. True to its name, this campground offers plenty of sites to escape to in its dark, wooded terrain. At the base of Berthoud Pass, far from the buzzing of the I-70 corridor, modern outlaws can find a bit of peace.

Robbers Roost is a spread-out campground in the tall timber at the western base of Berthoud Pass. RVs are not officially banned here, but the parking spots are smaller than most, and many sites simply cannot host a large rig. Robbers Roost is a tried-and-true Colorado mountain campground with a traditional "gather around the campfire in the pines" atmosphere. The dispersed arrangement is perfect for naturalists who don't like a strict layout or cookie-cutter feel at each campsite. The terrain allows for little room at each site and is suitable for small and midsize tents only. Level areas for tents are not in abundance, and it takes some time at each site to scope out the best place to lay your tarp—a refreshing change from the perfectly lined-up tent pads at some campgrounds.

Hike the Discovery Trail near Robbers Roost Campground.

Entering the campground and starting a counterclockwise loop, the road is visible from site 1, but sites 2–6, at the beginning of the campground, immediately eliminate the view of the highway. These five sites are the best in the campground because they are private and spacious. Sites 2 and 3 are best for space and flatness, while site 6 is the favorite because it is more private and at the end of a loop. A small stream passes these five sites, and site 6 even has a small footbridge you cross for campsite access. Site 8 offers less privacy since it's in the middle of the loop. Sites 7, 9, 10, and 11 are on the opposite side and uphill from the loop and are OK, but tent space is smallest at these.

Robbers Roost does get a little road noise from US 40, but this is a mountain pass, not a major interstate. This area also receives a huge amount of snow accumulation and typically opens in mid-June, depending on the conditions.

Never far from modern comforts, campers at Robbers Roost may also step out and hit the small mountain town of Winter Park. Winter Park and Mary Jane ski areas are just down the road and offer fun year-round, including mountain biking and hiking in the summer camping season. The nearby Moffat Road is an abandoned high-alpine railroad grade, now a dirt road open to cars and bikes. Moffat Road is a fun lung-buster of a mountain bike ride up to Rollins Pass and a great cruise down. For a milder walking adventure, park at the Bonfils-Stanton Foundation trailhead right across the entrance from Winter Park Resort. Walk along the Discovery Trail, take a left on Rose Crown, and return on Challenger for a gorgeous 2.5-mile walk on packed dirt and boardwalk trails. Hit up the town of Winter Park (only 10 minutes away from the campground) for great places to eat, shop, and even catch a movie.

The Sulphur Ranger District, composed of more than 400,000 acres in Grand County, Colorado, is surrounded by mountains, meadows, and lakes. To the west of Robbers Roost, the three lakes of Grand, Granby, and Shadow Mountain are fun for the day with a small boat or fishing pole. The Stillwater area next to Grand Lake has miles of trails for OHV enthusiasts.

To the east of Robbers Roost, the ski area on top of Berthoud Pass is permanently closed, but the region offers plenty of hiking and access to wildlife and wildflowers.

The 12,000- to 13,000-foot mountains above the campground make up the spine of the Continental Divide. The tiny Fraser River that starts in the valley, near Robbers Roost, grows to become the massive Colorado River and flows into the Pacific Ocean to the west.

In contrast, and in the magical allure of the Continental Divide, all precipitation on the other side of the ridge above the campground ends up in tributaries that feed into the Atlantic Ocean to the east. Avalanche shoots on this side of Berthoud Pass are always awe-inspiring, fun to locate, and less threatening during the summer camping season.

Robbers Roost Campground

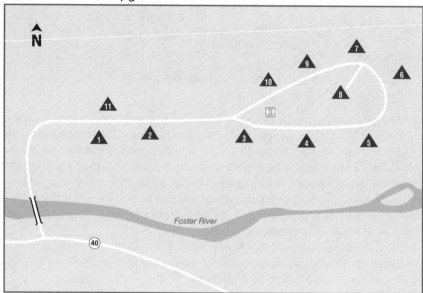

GETTING THERE

From I-70, take Exit 232 for US 40 headed toward Winter Park. Travel 21 miles to the base of Berthoud Pass, about 4 miles south of the Winter Park ski area.

GPS COORDINATES: N39° 48.350' W105° 44.383'

19

⚠ Rocky Mountain National Park: Aspenglen Campground

Beauty: ★★★★ / Privacy: ★★★ / Spaciousness: ★★★ / Quiet: ★★★ / Security: ★★★★★ / Cleanliness: ★★★★

One of your best bets for getting a good tent campsite in Rocky Mountain National Park

Aspenglen Campground lies just west of the town of Estes Park. Enter Rocky Mountain National Park immediately west of the Fall River entrance station. Here, the campsites are nestled among Douglas-fir, lodgepole pine, ponderosa pine, and the occasional Engelmann spruce, providing a nice mix of sun and shade. Grasses, shrubs, and seasonal wildflowers add lush texture and color to the open meadows.

This campground is hardly tent-only, but it's a wonderful family-friendly site where tents and RVs can coexist. Plus, a few walk-to tent sites provide seclusion for those who seek it. Wildlife is plentiful in the park: mule deer and the majestic Rocky Mountain elk are the most commonly spotted, although black bear, coyote, bighorn sheep, and moose inhabit the region as well.

Elk on Trail Ridge Road

Courtesy of Colorado Parks & Wildlife

KEY INFORMATION

LOCATION: Estes Park

INFORMATION: National Park Service, 970-586-1206, nps.gov/romo/planyourvisit/agcg.htm

OPEN: Year-round

SITES: 51 sites (14 tent-only, 6 walk-in)

EACH SITE HAS: Picnic table, fire grate, tent pad, food lockers

WHEELCHAIR ACCESS: Sites C30 and C31 are ADA-accessible.

ASSIGNMENT: By reservation; walk-ins permitted if sites have not been reserved

REGISTRATION: At recreation.gov

AMENITIES: Water spigot, flush toilets (no water late September–May)

PARKING: At campsites only

FEE: $30 per night, plus $25 park entrance fee

ELEVATION: 8,900'

RESTRICTIONS:

PETS: Must be leashed

QUIET HOURS: 10 p.m.–6 a.m.

FIRES: In fire grates only

ALCOHOL: At campsites only

VEHICLES: 30'

OTHER: 7-day stay limit per campsite

Earlier versions of this book promoted Timber Creek campground as the place to tent-camp in Rocky Mountain National Park. Not only was it friendly and peaceful, but it was also wooded and scenic. Unfortunately, this place has had its run of bad luck. It experienced nasty pine beetle infestation that wiped out much of the tree cover. Then, in 2020, it landed smack in the middle of Colorado's two largest wildfires to date. As of publication time, it was closed until further notice. Aspenglen takes its place.

The campground is divided into three loops: A, B and C. Loop A should be your first choice. There are five nice tent-only spots in this loop, but if you don't mind a walk, the best tent experience will be at the walk-in tent camping sites in Loop A: sites A, B, C, D, and E. All are 80–180 yards from the parking area, and most are right along Fall River.

There are three tent-only sites in Loop B, one of which is a walk-in site about 50 yards away. Most of the RVs end up in the last part of the C Loop, but there are six tent-only sites along the road to that loop. The two ADA-designated sites are in Loop C. Generators are allowed in Loop C, but only hours are restricted to 7:30–10 a.m. and 4–8:30 p.m.

The ranger on duty at the campground can steer you on a hike to meet your abilities and desires. Be sure to stroll the Aspenglen Campground Trail, which is just a quarter-mile walk between loops and stops at an amphitheater for summer educational programs. You can also stop in at the Fall River Visitor Center, which offers a wealth of information on what's open and nearby. Be prepared for some extended closures from the 2020 Cameron Peak and East Troublesome Fires.

Rocky Mountain National Park has more than 350 miles of hiking trails, so you're sure to find something that piques your interest and ability. You might try nearby Macgregor Falls Trail to the northeast, or check out the Deer Mountain out-and-back trail for excellent summer wildflower viewing. If they're open, don't miss driving Trail Ridge Road and Old Fall River Road. Trail Ridge Road is America's highest continuous highway. The historic Old Fall River Road, constructed in 1920, is a steep, switchbacking gravel road climbing from Horseshoe Park to Fall River Pass at 11,796 feet above sea level.

You might spot a beaver or two in Fall River. Wildlife is plentiful in Rocky Mountain National Park, from mule deer and elk to black bears, coyotes, bighorn sheep, and moose. Be sure to respect the animal and plant life here in Rocky Mountain National Park. If the recent wildfires have told us anything, it's how quickly this can all be taken away.

Rocky Mountain National Park: Aspenglen Campground

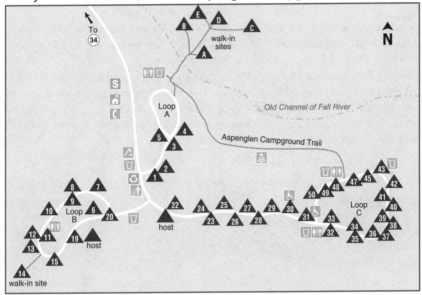

GETTING THERE

From Estes Park, follow US 34 W/Fall River Road 3.5 miles to Aspen Glen Campground, entering through the Fall River Entrance Station.

GPS COORDINATES: N40° 24.000' W105° 35.580'

Weston Pass Campground

Beauty: ★★★★ / Privacy: ★★★ / Spaciousness: ★★★ / Quiet: ★★★★ / Security: ★★★ /
Cleanliness: ★★★★

Weston Pass is one of the nicer U.S. Forest Service campgrounds in Colorado.

Named after the scenic break in the Mosquito Range, Weston Pass is worth the bumpy ride in. One look at the mountains of the Buffalo Peaks Wilderness will make you wonder why you didn't get here sooner.

Weston Pass has only 14 campsites that are large and spaced far apart beneath a forest of lodgepole pines and other evergreens. The ground cover is mostly smaller trees and assorted rocks and boulders. Landscaping timbers and short concrete posts have been tastefully laid out to keep cars and camping areas distinct. As a result, Weston Pass has a certain orderliness that makes it feel more comfortable.

The mountains of the Buffalo Peaks Wilderness greet you on the road to Weston Pass Campground.

KEY INFORMATION

LOCATION: Fairplay

INFORMATION: U.S. Forest Service, Pike-San Isabel National Forests & Cimarron and Comanche National Grasslands, South Park Ranger District; 719-836-2031; fs.usda.gov/psicc

OPEN: late May–early October

SITES: 14

EACH SITE HAS: Picnic table, fire grate

WHEELCHAIR ACCESS: No designated accessible sites

ASSIGNMENT: First come, first served; no reservations

REGISTRATION: Self-registration on-site

AMENITIES: Vault toilets; no water

PARKING: At campsites only; max 2 vehicles per site

FEE: $17 per night

ELEVATION: 10,200'

RESTRICTIONS:

PETS: Must be leashed

QUIET HOURS: 10 p.m.–8 a.m.

FIRES: In fire grates only

ALCOHOL: Permitted

VEHICLES: 25'

OTHER: 14-day stay limit

The South Fork of the South Platte River and a low ridge dividing this creek from Rich Creek surround the campground. Head along the main drive and admire the size of the campsites set back in the woods several feet from their respective parking areas. Notice the Ridgeview Trail splitting off between two campsites. The seven sites on the main drive give way to a loop road that offers secluded campsites that drop down toward the clearly audible creek. Sites 10 and 11, as well as 12 and 13, are quite close to one another. Beyond the campsites, a low, rocky ridge shades the campground in the late afternoon. Two vault toilets conveniently serve Weston Pass. This campground is gaining in popularity but rarely fills during the week.

For your evening leg-stretcher, take the Ridgeview Trail about a mile to an overlook on the point between the drainages of Rich Creek and South Fork. Note that this trail also connects you to the Rich Creek Trail, which dives into the heart of the Buffalo Peaks Wilderness. The forests here are primarily conifer and aspen, with some piñons and junipers on the higher slopes. You may spot some wildlife, from bighorn sheep to beavers. You probably won't spot as many humans, which can be a welcome respite from the nearby Front Range.

For a longer day hike near Weston Pass Campground, set off on an 11-mile loop by taking Rich Creek Trail up to Buffalo Meadows and picking up the Tumble Creek Trail (also called the Rough and Tumbling Trail) back down. This hike opens up to inspiring views of the surrounding mountains of the Buffalo Peaks Wilderness, including East and West Buffalo Peaks—which are actually highly eroded ancient volcanoes. While not fourteeners, they both exceed 13,000 feet and have definite treelines that you pass on the way to sizable rock faces you could scale with little difficulty. Take the Tumble Creek Trail beyond Buffalo Meadows to the headwaters of Rough and Tumbling Creek, then up to the pass where the Rough and Tumbling Trail starts to descend. Veer east first to West Buffalo Peak, then to East Buffalo Peak. Return to the Tumble Creek Trail and backtrack to the campground. This makes a very long day hike, so leave early in the morning, and bring lots of water for this adventure.

If you don't feel like walking to a view, make the drive up to 11,921-foot Weston Pass. Here, you can look north at a seemingly endless range of peaks. You can also stay down low and fish your way around the South Fork or other waters in the wilderness. Or you can simply stay and enjoy the subtle, relaxing beauty of Weston Pass Campground.

Weston Pass Campground

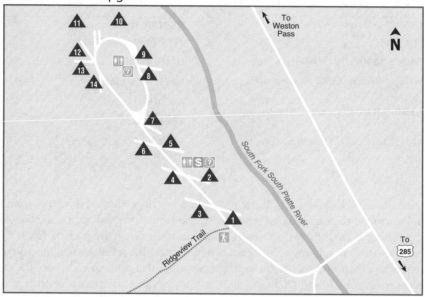

GETTING THERE

From the ranger station at the intersection of CO 9 and US 285 in Fairplay, drive south on US 285 for 4.8 miles and turn right onto CR 5 (Weston Pass Road). Continue on CR 5 for 7 miles and turn right onto CR 22. The campground will be on your left in 3.7 miles.

GPS COORDINATES: N39° 04.332' W106° 07.783'

21

⚠ Staunton State Park Campground

Beauty: ★★★★ / Privacy: ★★★★ / Spaciousness: ★★★★ / Quiet: ★★★ / Security: ★★★★ /
Cleanliness: ★★★★★

Escape to one of Colorado's newest state parks.

Opened in 2013, Staunton State Park honors the legacy of the Staunton family, who first settled here in the early 1900s. Rachel and Archibald Staunton were doctors who built their homestead over 80 acres of this land and provided medical care to Native American families and other homesteaders. Over the years, the Staunton land grew to 1,720 acres. The couple had a daughter, Frances H. Staunton, who later gifted the land to the state with the understanding that it would be transformed into a state park one day. After acquiring subsequent parcels, the state park now encompasses 3,828 acres of prime recreation land for locals and visitors.

One of the joys of camping here is that it feels a world away without being hours away. Located near Pine just off US 285, the campground is a mere 40 minutes southwest of Denver and only 6 miles west of Conifer. With grassy meadows and granite cliffs that soar to over 10,000 feet in elevation, the park offers varied geology; diverse wildlife; and a paradise for hikers, mountain bikers, and rock climbers.

Hike to your campsite at Staunton State Park Campground.

KEY INFORMATION

LOCATION: Pine

INFORMATION: 303-816-0912, cpw.state
.co.us/placestogo/parks/staunton

OPEN: Year-round

SITES: 25

EACH SITE HAS: Picnic table, fire ring,
bear-proof food container, tent pad

WHEELCHAIR ACCESS: No designated
accessible sites

ASSIGNMENT: Reservation only

REGISTRATION: 800-244-5613 or
cpwshop.com

AMENITIES: Vault toilets; no trash pickup

PARKING: The Meadow parking lot

FEE: $10 Parks Pass, plus $28 per night

ELEVATION: 8,215'

RESTRICTIONS:

PETS: Must be on a 6-foot leash and in your
control at all times

QUIET HOURS: 10 p.m.–6 a.m.

FIRES: No charcoal or wood fires allowed

ALCOHOL: Permitted

VEHICLES: In parking lot only

OTHER: No hammocks allowed; 14-day stay
limit in a 28-day period

The most appealing aspect of camping here is that all of the campsites are hike-in only. That means no RV camping, no trailers, and no huge groups. As a result, the area feels a little quieter, a little more peaceful, and a little closer to nature.

The campsites are spread among three loops: the Ponderosa Loop, the Spruce Loop, and the Aspen Loop. Park in The Meadow parking lot and be prepared to walk 180–799 yards to your campsite. The Ponderosa Loop sites are the closest to the parking lot, and most have partial shade and meadow views. Almost all of the sites in the Spruce Loop require a longer walk, and all are well shaded. The Aspen Loop falls somewhere in the middle. Site 20 offers a great view of Lions Head peak.

When I camped here with a friend, we chose site 19 in the Spruce Loop—the farthest site from the parking lot. While it required a few trips back and forth up the hill, the effort paid off with fewer interruptions from neighboring campers and a nice distance from the activity in the parking lot below.

While fires and charcoal grills are not permitted in the campground, propane and white gas stoves are allowed, so you can still have a hot coffee in the morning. The 12-by-24-foot tent pads can accommodate up to two tents each.

Staunton State Park offers nearly 30 miles of trails that you can explore by foot, pedal, or hoof. All trails are natural surfaces and vary in length and difficulty, from short 2-mile loops to daylong excursions. The trail to Elk Falls is popular with visitors, encompassing a 12-mile round-trip hike that stitches multiple trails together and includes a waterfall. You might also try the Historic Cabins Trail—an easy route through ponderosa pines, open meadows, and terraced gardens—for an up-close view of several of the homestead cabins, including the house built by the Staunton family in 1916.

One of the best things about this park's hiking trails is their accessibility. Staunton is one of the only places in Colorado offering Action Trackchairs, which give visitors with limited mobility the chance to explore three designated trails featuring views of Pikes Peak, Lions Head, and Mount Rosalie. At the time of publication, use of the Trackchair is free of charge (except for the required daily park pass).

Staunton is also a rock-climbing destination, and many climbers come to tackle the variety of routes on Staunton Rocks or Red Wall.

If you fish, you may enjoy dropping a line at the Davis Ponds, Elk Falls Pond, or one of the small streams in the park, where you can bank fish for rainbow trout or brook trout. Bring your current Colorado fishing license—but leave your boat at home.

Staunton State Park Campground

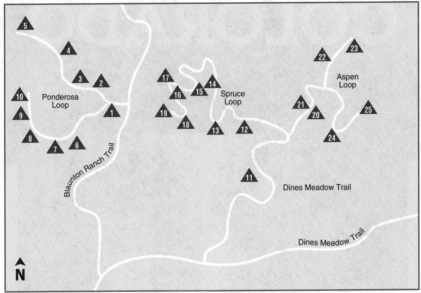

GETTING THERE

From Conifer, head south on US 285 south for 4.7 miles. Take the exit toward Elk Creek Road/Shaffers Crossing, and turn right onto South Elk Creek Road. Drive 1.3 miles, then turn right into Staunton State Park. The entrance station will be on your left.

GPS COORDINATES: N39° 29.813' W105° 22.927'

NORTHWEST COLORADO

Weir and Johnson Campground (see page 105)

22

⚠ Cold Springs Campground

Beauty: ★★★★ / Privacy: ★★ / Spaciousness: ★★★ / Quiet: ★★★ / Security: ★★★ / Cleanliness: ★★★★

Cold Springs is one way to have it all while camping in the eastern Flat Tops Wilderness.

Camping at Cold Springs is like checking all the boxes on everything you love as a tent camper. Camping near a bubbling cascade? Check. Camping near a mountain pond? Check. Camping by a spectacular mountain view? Double check. Add in camping next to Colorado's second-largest protected wilderness and you have what some would call a sheer earthly delight.

Now, this place isn't perfect, but it's pretty close. You can leave your tent, fish and hike all day, and then return to your little scenic mountain haven. Sure, it's a little closer to the road than is truly ideal, and the campground as a whole is pretty broken in. But if you're OK with those compromises, give this place a shot.

Turn into the short campground drive and check out the first campsite on your left, in an open meadow with the best of alpine views. Snow-covered Flat Top Mountain lies across Bear River, which rushes from Stillwater Reservoir above. Behind you, tree-covered slopes rise to mountain lakes. There is a good view down the valley of Bear River as well.

Fishing in the pond near Cold Springs Campground

John Dickson/U.S. Forest Service

KEY INFORMATION

LOCATION: Yampa

INFORMATION: U.S. Forest Service, Medicine Bow–Routt National Forests & Thunder Basin National Grassland; 970-638-4516; fs.usda.gov/mbr

OPEN: Mid-June–Mid-October

SITES: 5

EACH SITE HAS: Picnic table, fire grate

WHEELCHAIR ACCESS: No designated accessible sites

ASSIGNMENT: First come, first served; no reservations

REGISTRATION: Self-registration on-site

AMENITIES: Water, vault toilets, trash collection

PARKING: At campsites only

FEE: $10 per night

ELEVATION: 10,200'

RESTRICTIONS:

PETS: Must be leashed

QUIET HOURS: 10 p.m.–6 a.m.

FIRES: In fire grates only

ALCOHOL: At campsites only

VEHICLES: 22'

OTHER: 14-day stay limit

Cross over a small stream, then enter the small loop road. To your right is the mountain pond. Above it, on the hill, are two other streams noisily dropping over rocks into the pond. The second campsite lies in an open meadow next to the pond and the first stream. This is the largest and most popular campsite. The third campsite is close to the pond as well, with great views but no shade.

The fourth campsite is closest to the cascades and has some shade-providing spruce. The fifth campsite is set off in a forested corner of the campground beside a stream of its own. This is the shadiest and most private campsite—snag this one if it's available. An outhouse lies in the center of the loop, and a water spigot is convenient for all campers.

If Cold Springs is full—and with only five sites, it may very well be on a busy summer weekend—try Horseshoe Campground just a little way back down Bear River Road. It has seven campsites and is more forested than Cold Springs; consequently, it doesn't have the inspiring views. There's no camp host, but the host at Bear Lake Campground takes care of cleaning, trash removal, and fee collection.

The Flat Tops Wilderness is all around you: cliffs towering over alpine tundra and subalpine terrain, where spruce/fir forests give way to more than 110 fish-filled lakes and ponds. Another 100 miles of streams flow through this angler's fantasy land. Just a 5-minute jaunt up the road from Cold Springs is a major trailhead, Stillwater, leading into the Flat Tops.

To survey your kingdom for a day, take the North Derby Trail (1122). Cross the Stillwater Dam to a large park, then climb into the wooded highlands through a burned area, coming to an 11,200-foot pass after about 2 miles. Turn left at the pass, leaving the maintained trail, and stay on the divide, rising to the peak of Flat Top Mountain at mile 4. There is a rock pile at the 12,354-foot summit. Look down and see if you can spot your tent back at the campsite. You can also stay on the maintained trail and come to Hooper and Keener Lakes at 3 miles. These are great fishing lakes.

Bear River Trail (1120) leaves Stillwater Reservoir and goes west into the wilderness. Pass Mosquito Lake at mile 1.5, a scenic yet dubious destination, and then climb toward the high country. Once up high, you can go along the Flat Tops in either direction or drop down toward Trappers Lake. The high-country trails are fairly level, for scenic, mild hiking.

East Fork Trail (1119) splits off Bear River Trail and heads north into some superb vistas. Pass Little Causeway Lake at mile 1.6, then climb up toward the Devils Causeway, a side destination from the East Fork Trail. This is a narrow stretch (4 feet wide) of the Flat Top plateau that drops 1,500 feet in either direction. On the main trail, you will come to many small lakes and, finally, Causeway Lake at 5.7 miles. Anglers, be sure to bring your rods.

For those who want hike-free fishing, there are three reservoirs in the Bear River Corridor. The closest are Stillwater Reservoir, Bear Lake, and Yamcolo Reservoir. In between these reservoirs flows the Bear River. Anglers can be seen bank fishing the lakes and walking the meadows of Bear River. All these waters are stocked.

Limited supplies can be bought in Yampa. When you come to Cold Springs, expect to be busy—the great view at the campground will inspire you to be a part of the scenery.

Cold Springs Campground

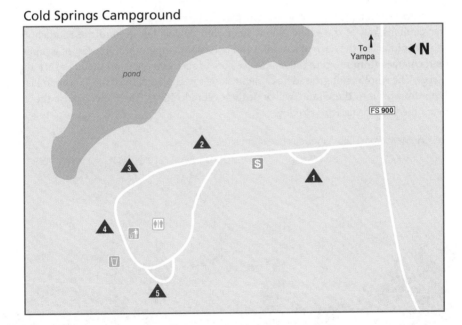

GETTING THERE

From Yampa, drive southwest on CR 7 for 7 miles to FS 900. Proceed on FS 900 for about 10 miles. Cold Springs will be on your right.

GPS COORDINATES: N40° 01.638' W107° 07.483'

23

⚑ Colorado National Monument: Saddlehorn Campground

Beauty: ★★★ / Privacy: ★★★ / Spaciousness: ★★★ / Quiet: ★★★★ / Security: ★★★★ / Cleanliness: ★★★★

Deep canyons, red rocks, and natural stone sculptures characterize this unique Colorado spectacle.

You can't talk about Colorado National Monument without tipping your hat to Jim Otto. In 1907, Otto came to the canyon country southwest of Grand Junction and deemed it the most beautiful place he had ever seen. He thought it worthy to be a national park; he single-handedly developed trails among the forests and rock sculptures while simultaneously promoting the land with a few converts from Grand Junction. Four years later, Colorado National Monument was established. Otto's devotion to the park persisted until 1927, when he relinquished his $1-per-month job as park caretaker. Otto had great foresight in protecting such a colorful landscape. Today you can enjoy it too.

Saddlehorn Campground is near many park features and hosts a few features of its own. After climbing out of the valley below, steer your vehicle left around the Saddlehorn (it really does look like the horn of a saddle) and enter the campground. A forest of juniper and piñon emerges from the rust-red soil. Occasional rocks emerge from the fiery dirt among the sage. The whole campground has a slight slope toward the cliffs of the Colorado Plateau, which drop off into the Grand Valley of the Colorado River. The views across the valley toward the Grand Mesa are striking.

Sweeping views from Loop A in Saddlehorn Campground

KEY INFORMATION

LOCATION: Fruita

INFORMATION: National Park Service, 970-858-3617, nps.gov/colm

OPEN: Loop A, year-round; Loop B, mid-March–mid-October; Loop C, when necessary; no water in winter

SITES: 80

EACH SITE HAS: Picnic table, stand-up grill

WHEELCHAIR ACCESS: Sites 5 and 70 are wheelchair accessible.

ASSIGNMENT: By reservation; walk-in permitted if sites have not been reserved

REGISTRATION: At recreation.gov

AMENITIES: Water, flush toilets

PARKING: At campsites only

FEE: $22 per night, plus $25 entrance fee

ELEVATION: 5,800'

RESTRICTIONS:

PETS: Must be leashed

QUIET HOURS: Generator use is prohibited from 8 p.m. to 8 a.m.

FIRES: No wood fires, charcoal fires in grills only

ALCOHOL: At campsites only

VEHICLES: 40'

OTHER: 14-day stay limit

The campground water spigots are tastefully piped into native stone, which adds a little extra touch to Saddlehorn. The junipers here are bushy; they provide decent campsite privacy, but the noonday sun will still beat you down in midsummer. My family and I came here in early June and just about abandoned ship because of the heat. Plus, the bugs can be a real pest that time of year. Aim for a fall visit.

Loop A has 20 sites that offer great views of the valley. Several of the sites are screened from the loop road. Loop B is very similar to Loop A and has some private sites and great views, plus well-maintained restrooms. From this loop, you can see the lights of Grand Junction shining below after dark.

Loop C is part of the original campground built in the 1930s. The campsites are a little smaller than what we are accustomed to today. This loop offers views of the valley and into the monument, but it is only open if the other loops are full.

Backcountry camping is also permitted in the monument. Obtain a free backcountry permit at the visitor center. Water is not available in the backcountry, so take plenty with you—especially in summer.

The best time to visit Colorado National Monument is mid-September–mid-November. The weather has cooled, the bugs are long gone, and the hiking is great. You can actually walk from your tent to some of the best day hikes in the park. Window Rock Trail makes a short loop and offers fantastic views. The Canyon Rim Trail travels on the edge of Wedding Canyon for more views. And views are what this monument is all about. Springtime is also pleasant and known for wildflower-viewing.

Another ranger recommendation is Otto's Trail. This gentle 1-mile round-trip trail leads through piñon/juniper woodlands and opens up to views of Sentinel Spire, Pipe Organ, Praying Hands, and Independence Monument. For something a bit longer, try the 6.5-mile Corkscrew Trail Loop, built by John Otto in 1909.

There are several longer trails. Monument Canyon Trail is 12 miles round-trip and enters the heart of the natural rock sculptures. This trail was improved in 2021. Also look for climbers scaling Independence Monument; if you're interested in joining them, stop at the park visitor center, which has a book on climbing routes.

If you need a break from the weather, use the middle of the day to make the 23-mile scenic (and air-conditioned) drive from one end of the park to the other. There are numerous overlooks—you might wear out your brakes stopping at all the dramatic canyon scenes. Road bikers also enjoy pedaling the scenic road, and the annual Tour of the Moon cycling event celebrates the jaw-dropping high-desert landscape. The combination of scenery against the backdrop of the plateau and valley country makes for one photo op after another. Rangers hold interpretive programs on summer weekends. However you spend your day, remember to be looking at the sky just before dusk; the sunsets (and sunrises) here are something to see.

Colorado National Monument is a destination in its own right. You'll definitely want to drive through if you are traveling along I-70—and if you have time to stay, the hiking, scenery, and sunsets will be worth it.

Colorado National Monument: Saddlehorn Campground

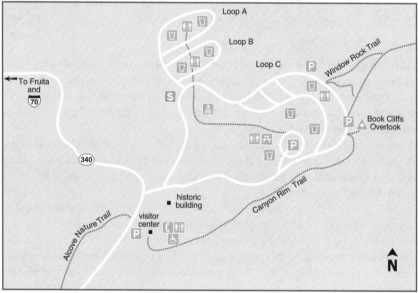

GETTING THERE

From I-70 in Fruita, head south on CO 340 for 2 miles to the Colorado National Monument entrance. Proceed into the monument for 5 miles, and Saddlehorn Campground will be on your left.

GPS COORDINATES: N39° 06.118' W108° 44.067'

24

Dinosaur National Monument: Echo Park Campground

Beauty: ★★★★★ / Privacy: ★★★★ / Spaciousness: ★★★★ / Quiet: ★★★★★ / Security: ★★★★★ / Cleanliness: ★★★★

This is one of the best tent campgrounds in the entire national park system, but you might need an all-wheel-drive vehicle to reach it.

The drive into Echo Park will amaze you, and the scenery will give you a feeling of tranquility. Rough going on the roads is both a blessing and a curse, as the sharp turns and steep grades tend to discourage large RVs.

Just the name of this place, Dinosaur National Monument, evokes a feeling of mystery and wonder. Echo Park is located in the heart of Dinosaur's canyon country, just below the confluence of the Yampa and Green Rivers. These waters flow around the massive Steamboat Rock. Colorful vertical canyon walls rise from across the river. The grassy meadow of Echo Park leads to another tan, gray, green, and black cliff face enclosing the park. A dense ribbon of box elder and cottonwood divides much of Echo Park from the river. The park continues upriver until the Yampa splits off to the right. Words can't begin to describe the true magnificence of Echo Park. You'll want to take your time getting here, both so you can safely navigate the road and so you can stop often to take photos. As you descend to the valley floor, you'll see a petroglyph site to the left and the turnoff for Whistling Caves to your right.

Peaceful campsites at Echo Park Campground

Eleanor and Vern Stockbridge

KEY INFORMATION

LOCATION: Dinosaur

INFORMATION: National Park Service, 970-374-3000 or 435-781-7700, nps.gov/dino

OPEN: May–September

SITES: 22

EACH SITE HAS: Picnic table, fire pit

WHEELCHAIR ACCESS: Site 1 is wheelchair-accessible.

ASSIGNMENT: First come, first served; 1 reservable group site

REGISTRATION: Self-registration on-site

AMENITIES: Vault toilets, drinking water available mid-May–late September; no trash collection

PARKING: At campsites only

FEE: $10 per night; $6 per night when water is turned off September–mid-May; park fee also required if you enter at the Dinosaur Quarry area on the Utah side of the park

ELEVATION: 5,000'

RESTRICTIONS:

PETS: Must be leashed; not allowed on hiking trails, on the river, or in the backcountry

QUIET HOURS: None

FIRES: In fire pits only. Bring your own wood (local firewood only); collecting wood from surrounding area is prohibited.

ALCOHOL: At campsites only

VEHICLES: RVs and trailers prohibited; all-wheel-drive and high-clearance vehicles recommended

OTHER: 14-day stay limit; limit of 8 people and 2 vehicles per site

---

Echo Park Campground is one of six campgrounds available in the park, with three on the Utah side and three on the Colorado side. It is off to the left, between the river and the meadow as you enter Echo Park. The spacious campsites are situated in a loop in the canyon bottom. Register near site 1, which is wheelchair accessible; this and site 2 are rather exposed but benefit from late afternoon sun.

The dirt road continues, then more campsites appear on the riverbank. Sites 3, 5, 7, and 9 are quite shaded and the most private. Sites 18, 19, 20, and 21 are designated for walk-in tent campers. Sites 10, 11, 12, 16, and 17 are situated against an impressive rock wall. The rest of the sites are closer to the inside loop. While there are no designated tent pads, there are plenty of flat options for staking your abode for the night. There is a water spigot (operational in summer) and two clean vault toilets.

You can count on getting a campsite during summer weekdays, but get to Echo Park early on summer weekends. Campsites are nearly always open during spring and fall. However, always call ahead to see if Echo Park is open, as rains can render the road impassable and close the campground.

On your way down Echo Park Road, enjoy the scenery of Sand and Pool Canyons, as well as an interesting Native American petroglyph site that was scratched high into the Sand Canyon wall. Whispering Cave is farther down, a great spot for a natural waft of cool air on a summer day.

The Green River will lure you to its banks, but the swift current can make swimming hazardous. Fishing is negligible for channel catfish, which inhabit the stained waters. The photographic opportunities are numerous, especially if you avail yourself of the numerous unimproved trails that leave Echo Park.

Mitten Park Trail leaves from the walk-in tent camping area and follows the Green River 1.5 miles to Mitten Park, a grassy meadow. You can also walk in the opposite direction along Confluence Trail, which heads toward Lower Sand Canyon in the shadow of Jenny Lind Rock.

Dinosaur National Monument offers much outside of Echo Park. About 27 miles west of Dinosaur, Colorado, in the state of Utah, is the Dinosaur Quarry Visitor Center Museum, which is overlaid on the fossilized bones of the dinosaurs that made this place a park. Harpers Corner Scenic Drive offers a worthy auto tour. Some awe-inspiring views can be found at the end of day hikes that spur off the scenic drive. Commercial outfitters offer rafting opportunities into the deep canyons of the monument as well. Once night falls, the exceptionally dark sky projects an incredible array of stars.

A camper we met who comes here every October suggested keeping mum about this special place. I understand why; such quietude and natural beauty are hard to find elsewhere. If you come here, make a commitment to keep it pristine. Pack out your trash. Be courteous. Keep it special for generations to come.

Dinosaur National Monument: Echo Park Campground

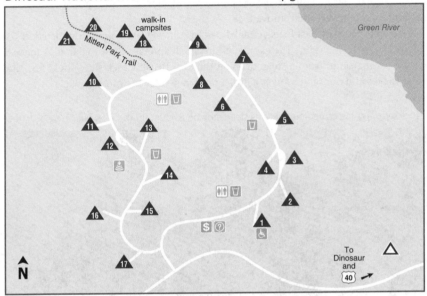

GETTING THERE

From Dinosaur, head east on US 40 for 1.5 miles to the Dinosaur National Monument entrance. Turn left on Harpers Corner Scenic Drive and follow it 25 miles to Echo Park Road. Turn right and proceed 13 miles, following signs for Echo Park.

Note: These roads are impassable when wet and are recommended for high-clearance vehicles only. Before heading to the Echo Park area, stop at the visitor center for information on road conditions or call 970-374-3000.

GPS COORDINATES: N40° 31.197' W108° 59.617'

25

Fulford Cave Campground

Beauty: ★★★ / Privacy: ★★★ / Spaciousness: ★★ / Quiet: ★★★★ / Security: ★★ / Cleanliness: ★★★

Fulford Cave offers attractions both above and below ground, as well as valley camping nearby.

Fulford Cave Campground is in an unusual setting, as it's one of the only places I've ever camped with access to a real-life bat cave.

The hilltop campground is on the east flank of the East Brush Creek Valley, in a scattered forest of aspen, spruce, and fir. Directly up the watershed is Craig Peak. Below you is the meadow of Yeoman Park—which actually had my preferred campground of the two, but as of 2022 Yeoman Park Campground was temporarily closed so that potentially hazardous trees could be surveyed and removed.

Drive up the bumpy East Brush Creek Road to Fulford Cave Campground, where a small spur road splits to the right. The campsites are small and clustered together. A fence separates the campground from a steep drop on the East Brush Creek side. These few sites are by themselves and out of view over a little knob; they offer the most privacy.

A fence separates the campground from a steep drop on the East Brush Creek side.

KEY INFORMATION

LOCATION: Eagle

INFORMATION: U.S. Forest Service, White River National Forest; 970-328-6388; fs.usda.gov/whiteriver

OPEN: April 15 (often later)–October 15

SITES: 6

EACH SITE HAS: Picnic table, fire pit

WHEELCHAIR ACCESS: No designated accessible sites

ASSIGNMENT: First come, first served; no reservations

REGISTRATION: Self-registration on-site

AMENITIES: Vault toilet; no water or trash collection

PARKING: At campsites only

FEE: $8 per night

ELEVATION: 9,400'

RESTRICTIONS:

PETS: Must be leashed

QUIET HOURS: 10 p.m.–8 a.m.

FIRES: In fire pits only

ALCOHOL: At campsites only

VEHICLES: 25'

OTHER: 14-day stay limit. All food and refuse must be stored in hard-sided vehicles or approved bear-resistant containers, or suspended at least 10 feet above the ground and 4 feet horizontally from any supporting tree or pole.

The other campsites are on a little loop road just as you pull up. There are no longer any potable water spigots at this diminutive campground. There's also no trash collection. Because of its small size and lack of amenities, as well as the narrow, rough road leading up to it, no self-respecting RV or pop-up camper would try to fit in these campsites. Just behind the campground is a beaver pond. Off to your left are the trailhead to Fulford Cave and the other trails leading into the Holy Cross Wilderness.

The main attraction here is Fulford Cave, Colorado's eighth-largest cavern. More than 2,600 square feet of the underground location has been plotted. Inside are big rooms, narrow crevices, streams, stalagmites (mineral formations rising from the cave floor), and stalactites (similar mineral formations that hang from the cave ceiling). Fulford Cave was discovered during the mining boom of the 19th century and was named after the nearby mining town of Fulford.

The 0.7-mile trail to the cave starts by the gate at the trailhead parking area. Start making your way up the forest on switchbacks, and you'll soon come to the cave. You can explore inside the cave, but you'll have to follow the rules. First of all, you'll need to submit a White River National Forest cave access registration form, which you can find on the U.S. Forest Service website. You'll also need to follow decontamination procedures outlined by U.S. Fish & Wildlife Service protocols before you enter any cave. This is to prevent spreading white-nose syndrome, a deadly wildlife disease that can be spread through clothing and equipment used in locales where the syndrome is found or suspected. Visit whitenosesyndrome.org to prepare for your trip.

Beyond these preparation measures, the Forest Service recommends you have the following with you: durable and warm clothing, gloves, a hard hat, flashlights and headlamps, sturdy boots, and drinking water. A cave map is available at the ranger station in Eagle. Remember, you are responsible for your own safety in the cave.

Above ground, there are two good trails that head into the Holy Cross Wilderness from Fulford Cave. The Lake Charles Trail follows East Brush Creek 4.1 miles before coming to the lake. You'll get an outstanding view of 12,947-foot Fool's Peak. Mystic Island Lake is half a mile farther. Both lakes offer good fishing for cutthroat trout, while East Brush Creek just below Fulford Cave offers fishing for rainbow and brook trout.

The Ironedge Trail is a horse and foot trail. It offers many highlights on its 7-mile journey, as the surroundings change from aspen to fir to alpine tundra above treeline. Along the way are cabins, meadows, and mine sites, interspersed with good views. The last 2 miles are downhill to Lake Charles. You can combine the Ironedge Trail with the Lake Charles Trail to make an excellent loop hike.

Before making a trip to this campground, check back to see if Yeoman Park Campground has reopened. I preferred it for its beautiful views of Craig Peak, wide-open meadow sites, and shady sites in the mature spruce forest. Sure, it caters more to RVs, but the experience, for me, was far more pleasant for an overnight.

Fulford Cave Campground

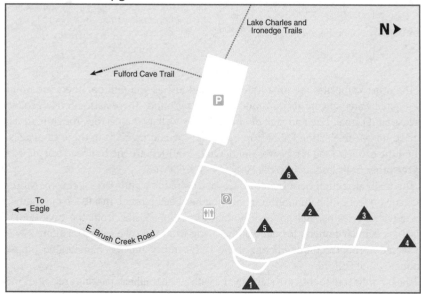

GETTING THERE

From I-70, take Exit 147 in Eagle, and head south on US 6 as it veers right and then makes a sharp left on Capitol Street. Proceed on Capitol Street as it turns into Brush Creek Road. In 10 miles, turn left on Forest Service Road 415 and follow it 7 miles to Fulford Cave Campground.

GPS COORDINATES: N39° 29.492' W106° 39.467'

26

Irish Canyon Campground

Beauty: ★★★★★ / Privacy: ★★★ / Spaciousness: ★★★ / Quiet: ★★★★ / Security: ★★ / Cleanliness: ★★★

If you really want to get away from it all, come to Irish Canyon. You'll see a whole different side of Colorado.

Irish Canyon is a place for adventurous tent campers—or simply those who seek true isolation. It is off the beaten path and then some, in the far northwest corner of the state, on Bureau of Land Management (BLM) land. This is in the Browns Park area, a place where Butch Cassidy and his gang retreated to safety between heists at the turn of the 20th century. Irish Canyon itself is named for a trio of robbers who lit down the gorge after a holdup in nearby Rock Springs, Wyoming.

These days, you can enjoy the scenery and solitude of Irish Canyon and then venture out to a host of sights, including 1,500-year-old petroglyphs, Vermillion Falls, Lodore Hall, Browns Park National Wildlife Refuge, the Gates of Lodore, and more. The abundance of regional geologic formations makes this place a geologist's dream.

As you enter Irish Canyon, you'll see high rock walls dropping down into sage, grass, and boulder fields. Gnarled old piñon and juniper trees rise along the wall in places. When you come to the campground, the sage gives way to old trees that climb up Cold Spring Mountain. Across the canyon is a sharp, high wall of rock, where small trees cling to precipices.

Marvel at the rock walls encircling Irish Canyon Campground.

Eleanor and Vern Stockbridge

LOCATION: Maybell

INFORMATION: Bureau of Land Management, 970-826-5000, blm.gov/visit/irish-canyon-acec

OPEN: April 15–November 30

SITES: 6

EACH SITE HAS: Picnic table, steel fire ring

WHEELCHAIR ACCESS: No designated accessible sites

ASSIGNMENT: First come, first served; no reservations

REGISTRATION: Not needed

AMENITIES: Vault toilet; no water

PARKING: At campsites only

FEE: None

ELEVATION: 6,650'

RESTRICTIONS:

PETS: Must be leashed

QUIET HOURS: 10 p.m.-8 a.m.

FIRES: In fire rings only

ALCOHOL: At campsites only

VEHICLES: 30', on roads only

OTHER: 14-day stay limit

The first site near the entrance overlooks the quiet road traversing the canyon, with ample space for a trailer but little tree coverage. The second site is more shaded. The campsites farther up the loop are more secluded and desirable. Site 3 provides the best shelter and privacy, and site 4 has the highest vantage point and adequate tree cover, even if the tent pad is slightly eroded. Sites 5 and 6 would be ideal for two parties wishing to camp near one another. A single, clean vault toilet lies in the wooded interior of the loop. Bring your own water and plenty of supplies.

This is a very isolated camp, but with a road alongside it. The area no longer hosts robbers; most passersby are friendly local ranchers, so you needn't be concerned about theft. Nor should you be concerned with Irish Canyon filling up. Campsites are available year-round.

A place like Irish Canyon is yours to explore and make your own adventures. There are no developed trails or brochures laying everything out. It is wise to contact the BLM office in Craig for information to help you plan exactly what you want to do.

On your way from Maybell, watch for signs leading to local sights, and make note of their particular roads. The old coke ovens are near Greystone. The Sand Wash Basin has a herd of wild horses. On the way in, stop at Vermillion Falls. It's a pretty yet strange sight—a cascade in such dry land. On old jeep roads, you can also explore Vermillion Creek and its colorful badlands canyon by foot or mountain bike. The Gates of Lodore is the entrance to a magnificent canyon, where the Green River leaves Browns Park and crashes downstream to meet the Yampa River at Dinosaur National Monument. A trail leaves the picnic area at the entrance of the canyon to see some Native American petroglyphs, a sampling of the rock carvings that exist all over this region.

The hiking and mountain biking around Irish Canyon is limited only by your stamina. Marked trails are few, but jeep roads are many. Below the canyon, paths lead up Green Canyon onto Peek-a-boo Ridge and a sweeping view of Browns Park below. Old jeep roads lead up Talamantes Creek farther up the canyon onto Cold Spring Mountain. Unless on foot, stay on the roads.

Drive almost to the Utah border, to Browns Park National Wildlife Refuge, to absorb a little human and natural history. Thousands of birds stop here during spring and fall migration. Elk and deer make this ribbon of green their home during the winter. You can make the 11-mile auto tour of the refuge and see the old Lodore Hall, where you'll find another petroglyph rock and the Two Bar Ranch. There's also two primitive campgrounds, Crook and Swinging Bridge, offering hiking, hunting, fishing, and wildlife observation year-round on a first-come, first-served basis.

This corner of Colorado captures a special part of the state that few people get to see. It's especially stunning in the fall. Bring water, supplies, and a sense of adventure, and you'll leave with memories to spare.

Irish Canyon Campground

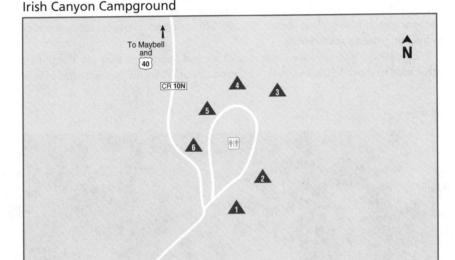

GETTING THERE

From Maybell, drive west on US 40 for 0.5 mile, then turn right on CO 318 and follow it for 41 miles to CR 10N. Turn right on CR 10N and follow it 8 miles to Irish Canyon Campground, which will be on your left.

GPS COORDINATES: N40° 49.735' W108° 44.142'

27

Rifle Falls State Park Campground

Beauty: ★★★★ / Privacy: ★★★★★ / Spaciousness: ★★★★ / Quiet: ★★★ / Security: ★★★★★ /
Cleanliness: ★★★★

Rifle Falls is the scenic centerpiece of the Rifle Valley. Set up your base camp here and explore the nearby parks and forest land.

You don't have to hike for miles to see one of Colorado's best waterfall sites. This one in particular was created from limestone buildup behind an ancient beaver dam, which made the cliffs we see today. The falls were a 19th-century tourist attraction and were then used as the impetus for Colorado's first hydroelectric plant. The plant was later dismantled, and a state park was built around the picturesque site. The state later renovated the park and campground into what we see today.

While the drive-in sites are convenient, they lack privacy as they are along the main tourist road to the falls. Instead, park your car at the small lot on the right after passing the

Rifle Falls, the centerpiece of the campground

KEY INFORMATION

LOCATION: Rifle

INFORMATION: Colorado Parks & Wildlife, 970-625-1607; cpw.state.co.us/placestogo/parks/riflefalls

OPEN: Year-round

SITES: 7 walk-in tent sites (Squirrel), 13 drive-in sites (Falls)

EACH SITE HAS: Walk-in sites have picnic table, fire grate, tent pad; drive-in sites have picnic table, fire grate, electricity.

WHEELCHAIR ACCESS: Site 2 is wheelchair accessible.

ASSIGNMENT: By reservation

REGISTRATION: 800-244-5613 or cpwshop.com, or the day you arrive, depending on availability

AMENITIES: Water, vault toilets

PARKING: At campsites or waterfall parking lot

FEE: $9 Parks Pass, plus $26 (basic tent campsite)–$36 (electric hook-up campsite) May–September; $22 (basic tent campsite)–$30 (electric hook-up campsite) October–April

ELEVATION: 6,500'

RESTRICTIONS:

PETS: Must be on 6-foot or shorter leash and cannot be left unattended

QUIET HOURS: None

FIRES: In fire grates only

ALCOHOL: Permitted

VEHICLES: No restrictions

OTHER: 14-day stay limit

---

fee station. Here you'll find the restrooms and water spigot. Then, take the wide, pleasant Squirrel Trail that runs along East Fork Rifle Creek. The first campsite, adjacent to the parking lot and set beneath tall narrowleaf cottonwoods, is the only site not along the creek. Continue on and you'll find more sites scattered among the box elder, willow, grass, and cottonwoods of the creek bottom. Site 16 looked particularly pleasant, with ample shade and sounds of the creek burbling below. Campsite 20 is a 10-minute walk from the parking lot. This site was recently relocated farther away from the trail for improved privacy from through-hikers.

All the sites have been renovated and are more appealing than ever. Each campsite is completely separated from the rest; the farther down the path, the more separated the sites become. The stream sends out a constant symphony of whitewater music. Squirrel Trail actually continues in a loop back toward the falls, but it's a tough scramble up the mountain for several minutes until you top out at Grass Valley Canal. From here, it's an easy service road walk to the falls parking lot. While it's an odd hike, there's plenty of wildlife.

Thirteen drive-in sites, which cater to RVs, comprise the balance of the campground. These sites have been renovated as well, and the whole campground has a tidy appearance that meets the high standards of Colorado state parks. Water spigots and new vault toilets have been built to serve the area. A camp host was on duty during our stay. You'll need a reservation no matter when you come, and the campground is open year-round.

Of course, Rifle Falls will probably be your first visit. Feel the mist as water plunges down three chutes to the pool below. Take the trail to the top of the falls and see the caves (and bats!) that are there too.

Farther up the valley is Rifle Mountain Park. Rock climbers from all over the world visit this park, scaling the sheer walls of the East Fork Rifle Creek canyon. In fact, the park has more than 250 bolted climbing routes, with a beginners area currently in progress. Even if climbing isn't your thing, check out the free show and admire their bravado. Anglers take note that the creek is stocked here. Farther up the creek is the White River National Forest. Another hiking opportunity is Three Forks Trail, which extends 5.3 miles from East Rifle Creek to the top of Coulter Mesa. This trail is also open to mountain bikers and horses and makes its way through several gulches and through blue spruce, Douglas-fir, and aspen forests. The trail is open to hiking, mountain biking, and horseback riding. A popular way to enjoy this trail is to hike or ride from top to bottom and arrange a car shuttle pickup.

Below Rifle Falls is Rifle Gap State Park. Boaters and Jet Skiers make wakes through the 350-acre impoundment, and there is a swimming beach for those who like their water sports a little slower. Try your luck and fish for rainbow and German brown trout, walleye, pike, smallmouth and largemouth bass, and yellow perch. Plus, Rifle Gap has a reputation as one of the state's best ice fishing destinations.

Harvey Gap State Park is just a few miles away and offers a peaceful, clear-water reservoir perfect for kayaking, paddleboarding, canoeing, and sailing (no water-skiing here). The 160-acre lake has trout and warm-water fish such as smallmouth bass and crappie.

The city of Rifle is nearby for any supplies you might need, so pitch your tent at the falls and enjoy the little Colorado valley that makes a big splash.

Rifle Falls State Park Campground

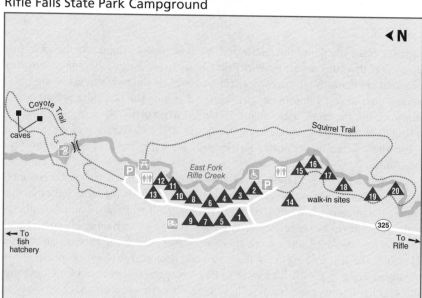

GETTING THERE

From Rifle, go north on CO 13 for 3 miles. Turn right onto CO 325 and drive 9.8 miles.

GPS COORDINATES: N39° 40.409' W107° 41.949'

⛺ Shepherds Rim Campground

Beauty: ★★★★ / Privacy: ★★★ / Spaciousness: ★★★ / Quiet: ★★★ / Security: ★★★★★ /
Cleanliness: ★★★★

This is the best tent campground at Trappers Lake, birthplace of the wilderness movement.

The Trappers Lake area is one of superlative beauty. This beauty is what spawned the wilderness movement as we know it today. In 1919, U.S. Forest Service employee Arthur Carhart was surveying the Trappers Lake area in order to lay out a road to and around the lake. He was to plot out some cabin sites on the lake. On seeing the beauty of the forest, water, and cliffs of this high country, he realized this was one place where humans simply couldn't improve on nature. He did complete the survey; however, he let his views be known to his supervisors that some natural places should be set aside in their original state.

At the time, this was considered radical thinking for the Forest Service. But it planted a seed. Years later, Congress passed the Wilderness Act of 1964 to preserve and protect certain lands "in their natural condition" and thus "secure for present and future generations the benefits of wilderness." Today there are more than 3.5 million acres of wilderness land set aside in Colorado alone, including the wilderness surrounding Trappers Lake.

The Trappers Lake area is stunning in the fall.

Eleanor and Vern Stockbridge

KEY INFORMATION

LOCATION: Meeker

INFORMATION: U.S. Forest Service, White River National Forest; 970-878-4039; fs.usda.gov/whiteriver

OPEN: Late May–early October

SITES: 16

EACH SITE HAS: Picnic table, fire grate, some tent pads

WHEELCHAIR ACCESS: No designated accessible sites

ASSIGNMENT: By reservation only

REGISTRATION: At recreation.gov

AMENITIES: Water, vault toilets, trash collection

PARKING: At campsites only

FEE: $20 per night

ELEVATION: 9,700'

RESTRICTIONS:

PETS: Must be leashed

QUIET HOURS: None

FIRES: In fire grates only

ALCOHOL: At campsites only

VEHICLES: 36'

OTHER: 10-day stay limit. Campground borders the wilderness; please obey all wilderness regulations.

The nearest wilderness, the Flat Tops Wilderness, nearly encircles Trappers Lake. There are several campgrounds in the immediate Trappers Lake area, but Shepherds Rim is the best for tent campers. Driving in, you'll see a dramatic burn scar from the Big Fish Fire of 2002, but the area is seeing slow yet steady regrowth. Shepherds Rim is set in a thin spruce forest. A slight slope has required the Forest Service to erect retaining walls and some steps between the road and the actual camping areas to level the campsites, making them more camper-friendly.

With 1 tent-only site and 15 standard sites, the layout of Shepherds Rim can accommodate RVs but caters mostly to tents and small campers. The abundance of tent pads means the majority of overnight visitors are tent campers. All sites are equipped with picnic tables and campfire rings. Guests also have access to vault toilets and drinking water. There are no electrical hook-ups. Most of the campsites are on the outside of the loop. Short paths connect parking areas to the picnic tables and tent pads.

Dramatic views of the Flat Tops Wilderness are available from various locations. Sites 7 and 8 have great views but are fairly exposed. Site 16 is especially desirable; large, sheltered and near the camp host. Sites 1, 3, and 5 are on the periphery with nice views below. Overall, this a well-kept, quality campground that you can use as a base camp to enjoy this area.

Water recreation centers around Trappers Lake, more than 300 acres of picturesque Flat Tops splendor. Cliffs rise above the forest, while brook and native cutthroat trout thrive in the waters. No motors are allowed here, so bring a paddle along with your canoe to enjoy the peaceful environment. You can also rent a boat from Trappers Lake Lodge. Only artificial flies and lures are permitted. Other fishing opportunities are along the North Fork of the White River below Trappers Lake and along Fraser Creek, which feeds Trappers Lake.

You can combine hiking and fishing by using many of the trails that radiate from Trappers Lake into the surrounding Flat Tops Wilderness. The nearest trail to Shepherds Rim is Wall Lake Trail (#1818). It leads up and away steeply from the campgrounds and immediately enters the former lodgepole pine and spruce forest area that was burned in the 2002

Big Fish Fire. The burned area continues until roughly 2 miles above Anderson Lake; use extreme caution among standing dead trees. Atop the plateau, the trail meets Oyster Lake Trail (#1825), providing access to the west. Roughly a mile past the Oyster Lake Trail junction, the trail reaches Wall Lake.

Carhart Trail (#1815) roughly circles Trappers Lake in a 4.5-mile loop. It parallels the east and north shores of the lake, allowing for angling opportunities, but pulls away from the lake on the west and south sides. The Carhart Trail provides access to the Little Trappers Trail (#1814) to the east, Trappers Lake Trail (#1816) to the south, and Wall Lake Trail (#1818) to the west.

Buy all your supplies before coming to Trappers Lake, then plan to stay awhile. This body of water and the surrounding Flat Tops are among the best locations in the state—and that is saying a lot.

Shepherds Rim Campground

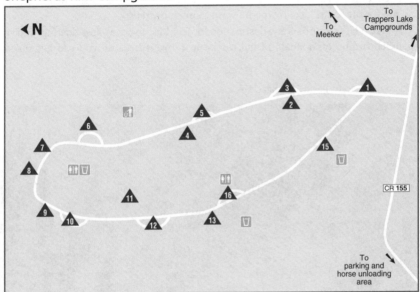

GETTING THERE

From Meeker, travel east 1 mile on CO 13. Turn right onto CR 8. In 38.7 miles, turn right onto CR 8A/CR 155/Trappers Lake Road. Travel 8.7 miles to the campgrounds. Turn right. Shepherds Rim Campground will be 1 mile on the right.

GPS COORDINATES: N39° 59.625' W107° 14.483'

29

Pearl Lake State Park Campground

Beauty: ★★★★★ / Privacy: ★★★ / Spaciousness: ★★★★ / Quiet: ★★★ / Security: ★★★★★ /
Cleanliness: ★★★★

This quiet, pristine lake offers proximity to Steamboat Lake and the resort town of Steamboat Springs.

The previous edition of this book listed Steamboat Lake State Park in this section, but when deciding between that and Pearl Lake State Park, I just couldn't leave out this jewel of a campground in the same vicinity. They both provide easy access to the town of Steamboat Springs—one of Colorado's most beautiful resort towns—as well as natural attractions like Hahn's Peak and the Mount Zirkel Wilderness. If you seek motorized boating opportunities, Fourth of July fireworks, a swim beach, and hot showers, then Steamboat Lake is your place. But for me, Pearl Lake is where I want to pitch my tent.

This lake offers a more serene destination for trout fishing, wakeless boating, and stand-up paddleboarding on a small, placid reservoir. I love it because you can get sites right

Reflect on the peaceful beauty of Pearl Lake.

KEY INFORMATION

LOCATION: Clark

INFORMATION: Colorado Parks & Wildlife, 970-879-3922, cpw.state.co.us

OPEN: Mid-May–October; yurt sites available year-round

SITES: 37 (including 2 yurt sites and host site)

EACH SITE HAS: Picnic table, fire grate, tent pad

WHEELCHAIR ACCESS: Site 35 and yurt site 6 are accessible.

ASSIGNMENT: Reservations strongly recommended

REGISTRATION: 800-244-5613 or cpwshop.com

AMENITIES: Vault toilets, flush toilet, water; yurt sites available. Shower, laundry, and dump station available at nearby Steamboat Lake State Park.

FEE: $9 Parks Pass, plus $24 per night ($90 per night for yurts)

ELEVATION: 8,100'

RESTRICTIONS:

PETS: Must be leashed

QUIET HOURS: 10 p.m.–8 a.m.

FIRES: In fire grates

ALCOHOL: None listed

OTHER: 14-day stay limit; 2-night minimum stay for yurts

near the water, if you're lucky; the lower loop has sites located 10–50 yards from the lake. Beyond the beauty of the lake itself, this well-maintained campground has many perks: level parking areas, large tent pads, drinking water, and both flush and vault toilets. As a bonus, Pearl Lake campers may use the shower, laundry, and dump station facilities at nearby Steamboat Lake State Park.

Another benefit of camping at Pearl Lake State Park is the ability to stay in a yurt. Two yurts are available for reservations year-round. Think of a yurt as an upgrade to a traditional tent. After all, they're inspired by the nomadic tents used in Mongolia and Siberia, stretched around wooden frames, with circular skylights for natural light. For $90/night, these yurts accommodate up to six people and offer electric heat and power, a table and chairs, two sets of bunks with double futons on the bottom, a picnic table, and a fire ring. Pets are allowed in yurt 16 ($10 nightly pet fee applies). Staying in one of these yurts in winter feels exceptionally remote, as they are accessible only by snowshoeing or cross-country skiing a half mile in. Note that there's no drinking water available at the yurts during the winter months.

If you do want to stay at Steamboat Lake, try the Harebell Loop in the Sunrise Vista Campground. There will be big rigs here, but this loop nevertheless offers the closest lakeside campsites at Sunrise Vista. The Larkspur Loop is well shaded. The other best option is on Bridge Island, on the far side of the loop, where there is a parking area for the tent-only campsites. These last 20 sites occupy the part of the island that juts out farthest into Steamboat Lake. The walk to the sites ranges anywhere from 20 to 200 feet; the lake and mountain views get better the farther you are from the parking area. The southernmost campsites are the best and most isolated. Boaters can actually pull their craft onto the shore of the island and walk to their campsite. The biggest downside is the exposure—there's barely any shade.

Steamboat Lake is, naturally, a park attraction. All manner of water sports are enjoyed on the lake. Skiers, anglers, and watercraft enthusiasts use the reservoir. A power zone and a no-wake zone make the lake enjoyable for all visitors. The inlets offer the best fishing for rainbow, brown, arctic grayling, and native cutthroat trout. If you didn't bring your own watercraft, anything from canoes to pontoon boats can be rented at the park marina, which also has limited supplies.

If you want to get around on foot, first hop in your car and enjoy the Routt National Forest, which nearly encircles Steamboat Lake. Hahn's Peak is a popular hike. The Mount Zirkel Wilderness is east of Steamboat Lake. The Slavonia Trailhead is your best bet for enjoying this glacier-carved highland, where hundreds of alpine lakes dot the landscape. Take the Slavonia Trail up to Gilpin Lake, then loop back down Gold Creek. The Encampment River and North Fork Elk River offer hiking and angling opportunities. Find maps and more information at the Steamboat Lake Visitor Center.

Pearl Lake State Park Campground

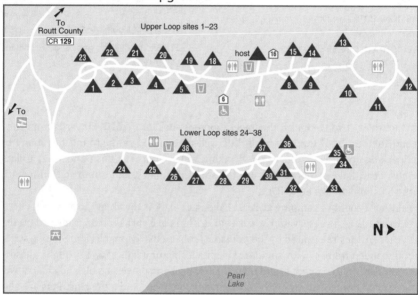

GETTING THERE

From Steamboat Springs, drive west on US 40 for 2 miles. Turn right on CR 129 and drive 22.4 miles. Turn right on CR 209 and drive 2.1 miles to the campground.

GPS COORDINATES: N40° 47.210' W106° 53.493'

30

⚠ Weir and Johnson Campground

Beauty: ★★★ / Privacy: ★★★ / Spaciousness: ★★★ / Quiet: ★★★★ / Security: ★★★ / Cleanliness: ★★★

Lakes are plentiful, and the camping is fine here on top of the Grand Mesa.

With an average elevation of more than 10,000 feet, the Grand Mesa is a cool island of green jutting up from the arid lands of western Colorado. There is a lot of blue too, with more than 300 lakes. There are several campgrounds up here, but a favorite is Weir and Johnson.

To begin with, Weir and Johnson is off the beaten path at the end of a side road, which makes for less auto traffic. That's important because when the snow melts up here, recreationists swarm the mesa like mosquitoes to the scenic lakes. You can't blame them. Once they see how pretty the waters are—rimmed by a spruce/fir forest and punctuated with flowery meadows—they keep coming back year after year, sometimes from many states away.

The small campground is situated between two reservoirs—the Weir and Johnson and the Sackett.

Christie Aschwanden

KEY INFORMATION

LOCATION: Grand Junction

INFORMATION: U.S. Forest Service; Grand Mesa, Uncompahgre, and Gunnison National Forests; 970-242-8211; fs.usda.gov/gmug

OPEN: Late June–late September

SITES: 12

EACH SITE HAS: Picnic table, fire grate

WHEELCHAIR ACCESS: No designated accessible sites

ASSIGNMENT: First come, first served; no reservations

REGISTRATION: On-site

AMENITIES: Vault toilets; no water

PARKING: At campsites only

FEE: $14 per night

ELEVATION: 10,500'

RESTRICTIONS:

PETS: Must be leashed

QUIET HOURS: 10 p.m.–8 a.m.

FIRES: In fire grates only

ALCOHOL: Permitted

VEHICLES: 22'

OTHER: 14-day stay limit

This campground also lies between two lakes (the Weir and Johnson and Sackett Reservoirs) and has trails leaving the campground to access three more. These lakes are in addition to countless other lakes, as well as the Crag Crest National Recreation Trail.

This is a small campground loop with clusters of Engelmann spruce and subalpine fir. As you reach the north side of the loop, there's a small parking area and a boat access path into the western tip of Weir and Johnson Reservoir off to your right.

As the loop curves, a small cascade rushes downhill past three excellent tent sites down from the loop road beside Sackett Reservoir. You have to carry your gear a bit to reach them (up to 100 yards), but you are that much closer to the aquamarine water. There are also two group sites, and the rest are back-in single sites with enough room for a small camper. The toilets were recently upgraded, but you must bring your own drinking water.

Call before you come here, as heavy snow can keep this campground closed well into July. Weekends can fill, but if you get here by midafternoon on Friday, you should be able to get a campsite. Campsites are nearly always available during the week.

Fishing is popular throughout the Grand Mesa. Trout swim the waters of the two campground reservoirs, but nearby hike-in lakes often see less fishing pressure. You can walk to Leon Lake from the campground. Just cross the Weir and Johnson Dam, hug the shoreline to the right, and cross a small pass to Leon Lake, which is larger than Weir and Johnson. In the opposite direction is the Sissy Trail to Leon Peak Reservoir, just 0.4 mile one way. It is all very pretty—wildflowers, lakes, pretty spruce forest. Bring a canoe or stand-up paddleboard if you have one. There is hardly more scenic paddling in the state.

Hiking The Crag Crest National Recreation Trail (aka The Crag) is tops for foot travel on the Grand Mesa. The 6.5-mile crest portion rides the spine of the mesa and offers views in all directions of far-off mountain ranges. On this inspiring hike, you can see all the lakes lying below you like emerald jewels in the forest. The loop portion of the trail passes through forest and meadow to complete a 10-mile circuit. You can pick up The Crag back on Forest Service Road (FS) 121 near The Crag Crest Campground, which you passed on the way in. Find more information at the Grand Mesa Visitor Center at the junction of CO 65 and FS 121.

Weir and Johnson Campground

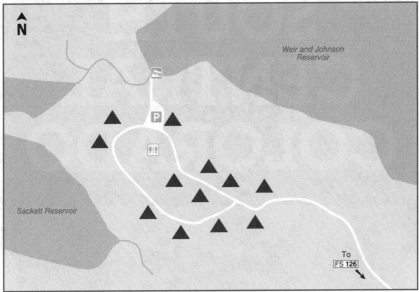

GETTING THERE

From Cedaredge, head north on CO 65 for 15 miles to FS 121. Turn right on FS 121 and follow it 9 miles to FS 126. Turn right on FS 126 and follow it 3 miles to dead-end at Weir and Johnson Campground.

GPS COORDINATES: N39° 04.015' W107° 49.883'

SOUTH CENTRAL COLORADO

A trail through the aspens near O'Haver Lake Campground (see page 121)

31

Alvarado Campground

Beauty: ★★★★ / Privacy: ★★★★ / Spaciousness: ★★★ / Quiet: ★★★★ / Security: ★★★★ / Cleanliness: ★★★★

A hiker's haven on the eastern slope of the Sangre de Cristo Mountains

Alvarado is a campground for all but especially the active set. Any given day there will be hikers, bikers, and horseback riders gearing up and heading out on their favorite trails. Several trails leave directly from the campground, which is a nice place to return after a day soaking up the scenic Sangre de Cristo Mountains.

On a slope just into the forest line above the Wet Mountain Valley, Alvarado Campground enjoys a mixture of woodland and meadow, where Douglas-fir and ponderosa pines intermingle with aspens. Dense cottonwood and brush grow along Alvarado Creek. Forest density varies with exposure throughout this campground. There are many options for both sun and shade, and the campground still has about 20 first-come, first-served sites in case you don't snag a reservation.

Alvarado is perched on the side of the Sangre de Cristo Mountains among sweet-smelling ponderosa pine, aspen, lodgepole, and Gambel oak trees. Some sites offer views of the Wet Mountain Valley below, while others sit beside Alvarado Creek. The campground is within reach of the Sangre de Cristo Wilderness, which spans 226,455 acres with 60 alpine lakes, 400 miles of streams, and more than 400 miles of trails to explore. Large aspen stands visible in the area today are the result of fires set in the early 1900s to clear pastureland, expose minerals, and produce charcoal.

A mix of trees, meadows and distant peaks at Alvarado Campground

KEY INFORMATION

LOCATION: Cañon City

INFORMATION: U.S. Forest Service; Pike–San Isabel National Forests & Cimarron and Comanche National Grasslands; 719-269-8500; fs.usda.gov/psicc

OPEN: Late May–Sept. 20

SITES: 47

EACH SITE HAS: Picnic table, fire grate

WHEELCHAIR ACCESS: Accessible outhouses

ASSIGNMENT: First come, first served for some, reservations required for 27 sites

REGISTRATION: Self-registration on-site, or reserve at recreation.gov

AMENITIES: Water, vault toilets, trash collection, equestrian sites

PARKING: At campsites only; limit of 2 vehicles per site

FEE: $22 per night

ELEVATION: 9,000'

RESTRICTIONS:

PETS: Must be leashed at all times

QUIET HOURS: 10 p.m.–6 a.m.

FIRES: In fire rings only

ALCOHOL: At campsites only

VEHICLES: 35'

OTHER: 14-day stay limit

Alvarado Campground is divided into three distinct areas. The lower level accommodates tents and RVs; each site has a tent pad and lantern post, but many are without shade or much privacy. The upper level is a prime destination for tenters, with walk-in tent campsites and far fewer big rigs. A portion of the middle section caters to equestrian campers with more space but no corrals. You must bring only certified weed-free hay, or certified weed-free cubes or pellets.

The first few campsites, 1–9, are in a meadow overlooking the mountains across the valley, then the main road enters a ponderosa grove. If you take a right into the equestrian camping loop, you can find a footpath that takes you to the Comanche/Venable Trailhead, with trails open to hikers, bikes, dogs and horses.

The main campground road splits into two at an oval-shaped loop with about a dozen campsites around it. Then, the road switchbacks farther up the mountain with more shaded and isolated campsites, and finally comes to a set of five walk-in, tent-only sites. Here, you park your car and walk a short distance to set up camp. Be aware that these sites are on a grassy slope, making it hard to find a level place to pitch your tent. Plus, there's less shade here. However, the entire campground is suitable for tents. This road ends at a turnaround and the Alvarado Trailhead, with partially paved trail access to Rainbow Trail, Comanche Lake Trail, and Venable Lakes Trail.

Water spigots and vault toilets are spread throughout the campground. Many of the sites are spread quite far apart. A campground host with a friendly dog and firewood for sale is stationed near the entrance to the campground.

A variety of recreational opportunities are within campers' reach. All trails are open for horseback riding and hiking, with some open to motorized vehicles, including Rainbow Trail. The non-motorized Comanche and Venable Trails lead into the Sangre de Cristo Wilderness, where waterfalls and alpine lakes abound.

Hikers, bikers, and equestrians all enjoy the nearby trails, most of which lead into the far-flung Sangre de Cristo Wilderness. The Comanche Trail heads up along Alvarado Creek to Comanche Lake. The Venable Trail leads up a couple of miles to Venable Falls, then a few more miles to the Venable Lakes areas. Some of these lakes are frozen until late June. You can combine the Comanche and Venable Trails and make a 13-mile loop via Phantom Terrace back to the campground.

Want to stretch your legs but not climb straight uphill? The Rainbow Trail runs 46 miles all the way from south of Alvarado north to Salida. You can use the Rainbow Trail to connect to other trails entering the Sangre de Cristo Wilderness. The Godwin Trail climbs to alpine lakes. The Cottonwood Trail climbs along Cottonwood Creek. Any of these bodies of water are suitable for fishing.

You can also drive to within a quarter mile of Hermit Lake, another alpine body of water high in the mountains. Take County Road 160 (Hermit Road) west out of Westcliffe and drive 13 miles to a signed parking area near the lake. Bring your fishing pole.

Reward yourself after all that exercise with a good meal at the Alpine Lodge, located a few steps from the campground. This is also a great place to book a cabin if you're past your tent camping days. Or you can drive into Westcliffe and take a walking tour of the quaint downtown area or load up on food, drink, and supplies.

Alvarado Campground

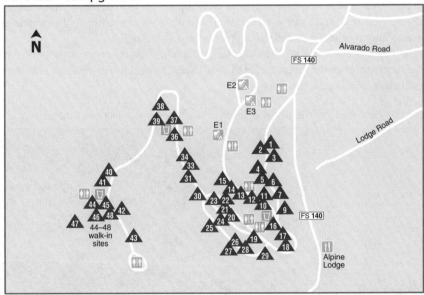

GETTING THERE

From the courthouse in Westcliffe, drive south on CO 69 for 3 miles to CR 140 (Schoolfield Road). Turn right on CR 140 and follow it 6 miles to Alvarado Campground.

GPS COORDINATES: N38° 04.762' W105° 34.082'

32

⛺ Bear Lake Campground

Beauty: ★★★★ / Privacy: ★★ / Spaciousness: ★★★ / Quiet: ★★★★ / Security: ★★★★ / Cleanliness: ★★★★

Though this relatively isolated campground in the San Isabel National Forest is gaining in popularity, it makes a worthwhile getaway, with the magnificent Sangre de Cristo Mountains providing a scenic backdrop for Bear Lake.

The snowy, granite domes of the Sangre de Cristo Mountains plunge down to a forest of spruce and fir. This in turn gives way to an open meadow and Bear Lake, where you can enjoy tent camping in the southeasternmost slice of national-forest land in Colorado. Fishing comes naturally here, and there are many stunning hiking trails in the vicinity, plus a side trip to the Spanish Peaks, a National Natural Landmark.

The campground is well placed next to the dense forest and mountain meadow above Bear Lake. Along the campground's gravel loop, several wooded campsites on the southeast side of the loop offer obscured views of Bear Lake. More-open sites with occasional stray aspens are in the center of the loop as the road swings around into the grassy meadow. What these campsites lack in privacy they make up for in views of Steep Mountain above, the nearby meadow, and a cathedral of peaks beyond. A few campsites on the outside of the loop face into the clearing, which has a stream flowing through it.

The Indian Trail starts just beyond the campground. Another creek rushes from the high country through the campground to Bear Lake. The next few campsites are in the spur to your right, offering the most privacy.

Take a side trip to the Spanish Peaks while staying at Bear Lake Campground near La Veta.

Paul Alhadef/Shutterstock

KEY INFORMATION

LOCATION: La Veta

INFORMATION: U.S. Forest Service; Pike–San Isabel National Forests & Cimarron and Comanche National Grasslands; 719-269-8500; fs.usda.gov/psicc

OPEN: Early June–mid-October

SITES: 14

EACH SITE HAS: Picnic table, fire grate, trash collection

WHEELCHAIR ACCESS: Only outhouses are specifically ADA-accessible

ASSIGNMENT: Reservations can be made for sites 2, 3, 4, 5, 6, 7, and 8

REGISTRATION: Self-registration on-site

AMENITIES: Pump well water, vault toilets

PARKING: At campsites only; limit of 2 vehicles or 1 RV

FEE: $21 per night

ELEVATION: 10,500'

RESTRICTIONS:

PETS: Must be leashed

QUIET HOURS: 10 p.m.–8 a.m.

FIRES: In fire grates only

ALCOHOL: At campsites only

VEHICLES: 40'

OTHER: 14-day stay limit; max 8 people per site. Friday and Saturday night minimum required stay on weekends; 3 nights minimum on holiday weekends. Walk-ups are exempt from the nightly minimum.

This is one of the highest campgrounds around, so bring that extra blanket and expect to find temperatures around, or possibly below, freezing throughout the summer. Since you're at 10,500 feet, be sure to cover yourself from the penetrating rays of the sun. Be prepared for windy, cool conditions anytime at Bear Lake. Stake your tent down well, because the gusts of wind from the peaks above can blow mighty strong. And finally, be bear-aware. In 2021, food lockers were installed at each campsite, helping deter the local residents bears that tend to patrol these grounds for fish or the leavings of careless campers.

Two vault toilets are located at the center of the loop and near the Indian Trail. An old-fashioned hand pump at the height of the campground provides water, which is tested each month. For your safety and security, a campground host is situated at the beginning of the loop during the summer season. Bring what you need so you don't have to leave this haven for a nearby grocery store.

Half of the sites at this campground are first come, first served, but the secret is out about Bear Lake; don't rely on any availability Thursday–Sunday. If the summer crowds are too much for you, consider coming late in the season. The campground stays open for mid-season hunters well into November, depending on the weather, so you could camp here for no fee—and without water, trash collection, and a host—if that floats your boat. Blue Lake campground is another option, as is Purgatoire Campground, an equestrian-friendly spot straddling the North Fork of the Purgatoire River.

After setting up camp, why not check out Bear Lake? A foot trail circles the deep-blue water fed by streams from above. Drop in a line or two; the lake is stocked each summer, typically with a rainbow hybrid. No luck? Try Blue Lake. Take the hiker-only to the almost equally scenic fishing waters. Whether or not you plan to fish, this is a spectacular walk on a well-marked trail with plenty of opportunities for wildlife-viewing. For anglers who prefer moving water, try fishing Cuchara Creek. It winds along Forest Service Road (FS) 422, your route up to Bear Lake.

Hikers have a few nearby options in addition to Bear and Blue Lakes. Take the Indian Trail from the campground north to Bonnett Creek, or make a loop via Dodgeton Trail and Baker Trail. Ambitious hikers will want to take the 3.5-mile gut buster up the four-wheel-drive road to Trinchera Peak (13,517'). The view will get your heart pumping again. This trek starts near Blue Lake.

Another option is driving from Bear Lake Campground back out to CO 12 along a portion of The Highway of Legends Scenic and Historic Byway to Cuchara Pass. You'll see volcanic formations as you ascend along the shoulder of the Spanish Peaks, which the Tarahumara Indians believed to be the origin of all life on earth.

Follow FS 415 from the pass to the Spanish Peaks. These two granite domes are an offshoot of the Sangre de Cristo Mountains and will deliver scenery overload if you head to and beyond Cordova Pass at 11,000 feet. This is a rough road, so take caution especially in the shoulder season. A high-clearance, four-wheel-drive vehicle is recommended.

Bear Lake Campground

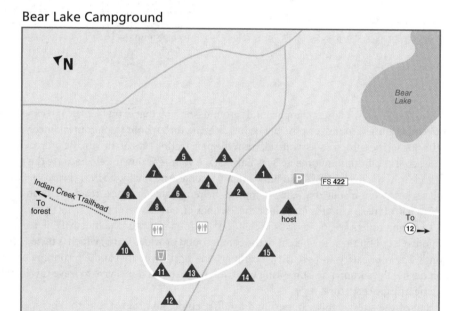

GETTING THERE

From La Veta, drive south on CO 12 for 15 miles. Turn right on FS 422 and follow it 5 miles to Bear Lake Campground.

GPS COORDINATES: N37° 19.542' W105° 08.600'

33

⛺ Great Sand Dunes National Park & Preserve: Piñon Flats Campground

Beauty: ★★★★ / Privacy: ★★★ / Spaciousness: ★★★ / Quiet: ★★★ / Security: ★★★★★ /
Cleanliness: ★★★★★

America's largest sand dunes perched against the Rocky Mountains is a sight to behold. Come see for yourself.

When I think about the Sand Dunes, I try to imagine what they must have been like hundreds of years ago. Were dust and sand still blowing across the San Luis Valley? Could our ancestors see Blanca Peak towering on the right? Were there swirling swaths of sand contrasting with the verdant Sangre de Cristo Mountains in the background? This incredible sight in the middle of the Rocky Mountains is certainly a wonder to behold, and camping here is a fantastic way to take it all in.

Piñon Flats Campground, located in the Great Sand Dunes National Park & Preserve, offers the closest established campsites to the dunes. This campground is set between the dunes and the high country in a juniper and pine forest with a sagebrush and grass understory. There are two long, narrow loops, each with a variety of campsites for tents or RVs. The Dunes Trail and seasonally flowing Garden Creek bisect the Piñon Flats.

A view toward the dunes at Piñon Flats Campground

KEY INFORMATION

LOCATION: Mosca

INFORMATION: National Park Service, 719-378-2312, nps.gov/grsa

OPEN: Year-round

SITES: 88

EACH SITE HAS: Picnic table, fire grate, tent pad

WHEELCHAIR ACCESS: Sites 10, 14, 51, and 63 and site C of the Group Loop

ASSIGNMENT: First come, first served and by reservation

REGISTRATION: 877-444-6777 or recreation .gov, or self-registration on-site. Camping permit required.

AMENITIES: Water, flush toilets, community sinks

PARKING: At campsites only

FEE: $20 per night

ELEVATION: 8,200'

RESTRICTIONS:

PETS: Must be leashed

QUIET HOURS: None

FIRES: In fire grates only

ALCOHOL: At campsite only

VEHICLES: 35'

OTHER: 6 people maximum per site; 14-day stay limit

Loop 1 is lower and closer to the dunes. A paved road cuts down on dust. Low stone walls level the ground and define boundaries between the loop's 44 campsites. Large rocks keep cars where they are supposed to be. Some campsites are nestled in piñon thickets; others are more open but offer views of the dunes and mountains. Most sites are spacious. As the loop circles back, campsites drop down from the road toward the dunes. These sunny sites offer incredible views of the sands, but they have a more worn and dusty appearance.

Loop 2 parallels Loop 1 but is situated on higher, more wooded ground. It has 44 campsites as well, and a few cottonwoods grow alongside Garden Creek, breaking up the evergreens. Elaborate rockwork keeps the natural areas from being trampled and levels the campsites. Just beyond the Dunes Overlook Trail is a set of sites that offer great views of the contrasting sand dunes and mountains.

Each loop has two comfort stations with flush toilets, drinking water, and sinks for washing your dishes. Between Loop 1 and Loop 2 is a small store that is open between May and September. It offers typical camp supplies, such as ice, wood, and soda. I suggest making a major supply run before you get to the dunes, but if you run out of something, you can buy it here.

Piñon Flats fills up in the summer—on both weekends and weekdays. Grab a reservation as early as you can. However, don't discount a fall visit. From September to May, the campground is quiet and campsites are more readily available. Late spring and early fall are the best times to visit.

One of the great things about this national park is its accessibility. A wheelchair-accessible mat offers access from the dunes parking area to the edge of Medano Creek and the sand. To go farther, go to the visitor center to request a sand wheelchair, designed with large inflatable tires to make short trips across the sand.

While you're here, you're likely to wonder what's it like to stand atop a 700-foot sand dune. Here's your chance to find out. Take the half-mile Dunes Trail from the campground down to the dunes and start climbing. The loose sand and deceptive distances make it more challenging than you may have expected. This is one place where your footprints never last for long.

Eighteen miles of more foot-friendly trails lace the park. Head north from the campground on the Dunes Overlook Trail 1.2 miles to a cliff overlooking the dunes. The Wellington Ditch Trail is an easy hike, less than 1 mile one-way, along an old settler's irrigation flow. Add about 0.5 mile for a stroll around the Nature Trail Loop and on to the visitor center. The high country awaits you on the Mosca Pass Trail.

In the summer, there are ranger-led walks every day and programs every evening. The ever-changing light and shifting dunes combine to present an evolving landscape as you explore the environment. Simply being here, at the largest sand dunes in North America, is a rewarding experience.

Outside the park is a short walk to Zapata Falls. It is on public land a few miles south of the monument on CO 150. Step gingerly among the rocks and feel the cold mist of the falls for a nice break from the summer heat. You can extend the hike 3 more miles up to alpine Zapata Lake. Nearby San Luis Lakes State Park offers fishing, boating, and wildlife-viewing. Thousands of acres of the Sangre de Cristo Wilderness lie east of the dunes. And for something even more unusual, stop by Colorado Gators Reptile Park, an alligator and reptile refuge that adds a bit of adventure to an already fascinating part of the state.

Great Sand Dunes National Park & Preserve: Piñon Flats Campground

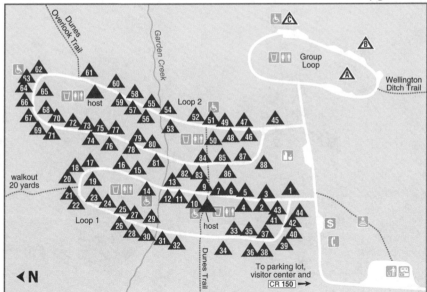

GETTING THERE

From Blanca, drive west on US 160 for 5.2 miles. Turn right on CO 150 and follow it 16 miles to Great Sand Dunes National Monument.

GPS COORDINATES: N37° 44.782' W105° 30.283'

34

⚠ East Ridge Campground

Beauty: ★★★ / Privacy: ★★★★ / Spaciousness: ★★★ / Quiet: ★★★★ / Security: ★★★★ /
Cleanliness: ★★★★

Pitch your tent near one of Colorado's prehistoric wonders.

East Ridge Campground is such a special find. Here, you can camp where dinosaurs roamed more than 100 million years ago and within footsteps of the Royal Gorge—the 10-mile-long, nearly 1,000-foot-high chasm for which this region is known. The Royal Gorge Bridge was constructed in 1929 and remains one of the most popular places to visit.

In fact, the Royal Gorge region sees approximately 2.3 million visitors per year. This Central Colorado destination just 2 hours from Denver features jaw-dropping scenery, heart-pumping recreation, and great local businesses. Most people opt for a hotel or

Camp on the south branch and watch the clouds roll in over Cañon City.

KEY INFORMATION

LOCATION: Cañon City

INFORMATION: City of Cañon City, 800-704-6743, royalgorgeregion.com/camping

OPEN: Year-round

SITES: 23

EACH SITE HAS: Tent pad, fire ring, picnic table

WHEELCHAIR ACCESS: No designated accessible sites

ASSIGNMENT: First come, first served; no reservations

REGISTRATION: On-site

AMENITIES: Vault toilets; no water

PARKING: At campsites only

FEE: $20

ELEVATION: 6,300'

RESTRICTIONS:

PETS: Must be leashed

QUIET HOURS: None

FIRES: In fire rings only

ALCOHOL: Permitted

VEHICLES: No restrictions

OTHER: 14-day stay limit

bed-and-breakfast during their visit. Lucky for us tent campers, most people also seem to overlook nature's accommodations just 10 miles west of Cañon City.

East Ridge Campground is just one of seven primitive campgrounds this region has to offer. East Ridge is my favorite because of its location—perched on a bluff where you can watch the sunset over the gorge to the west and peer down at the lights of Cañon City to the east. It's charming in its simplicity, and on a Thursday night in August, a friend and I had it almost to ourselves.

The 23 newly constructed designated campsites are fairly well spaced out, although none are exceptionally private. The campground is divided into two primary branches, one to the south and one to the north. The south road runs along a ridge with views of Cañon City to the east. It's only a short hike west from your campsite to the gorge rim. The north road feels more clustered. Most of the sites can accommodate big trailers and RVs, but this place doesn't usually get the loud or rowdy types. Here, RVers and tenters seem to coexist in peace. Many of the fire rings are nestled within rock retaining walls.

The Canyon Rim Trail, among others, is a short walk from camp. We hiked the 1.6-mile stretch in the early evening, passing piñon, juniper, and cactus and arriving at several spots to peer over the rim to the river far below—an inspiring and exceptionally private view of the main attraction in this region. Hook up with the dirt road to walk back and ponder the view and whatever you plan on eating for dinner. Another nice walk is the S'Mores Trail, which is a half-mile jaunt top to bottom and a nice way to get the lay of the land of East Ridge Campground. You can make a long loop connecting the Cañon Vista Trail with the FAR Out trail, returning on the Canyon Rim Trail.

When you wake up in the morning, the world is your oyster. From traversing the dizzyingly high Royal Gorge Bridge to off-roading on a Jeep tour to whitewater rafting through the Arkansas River below, there's so much to do. You can plan your adventure online at royalgorge.info straight from your smartphone while settling into your campsite at night, since you'll likely have cell service.

East Ridge Campground

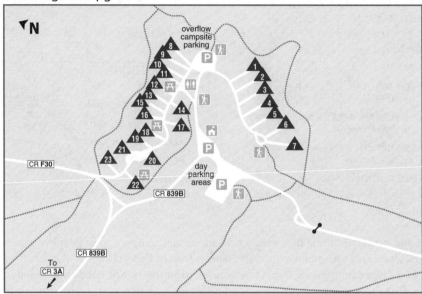

GETTING THERE

From Cañon City, take US 50 west nearly 12 miles to CR 3A. Turn left and drive 2.5 miles. Stay left at the fork to get on CR F30, and drive another 1.5 miles. Turn left at CR 398B and follow signs into East Ridge Campground.

GPS COORDINATES: N38° 27.896' W105° 17.606'

35

O'Haver Lake Campground

Beauty: ★★★★ / Privacy: ★★ / Spaciousness: ★★★ / Quiet: ★★★ / Security: ★★★ / Cleanliness: ★★★★

Lakefront camping in the heart of South Central Colorado

I admit that I waffled over whether to include O'Haver Lake Campground in this book. It might be because, on my visit, the place was swarming with both RVs and wasps. Both put a damper on my experience. But looking back, camping at O'Haver Lake Campground had many beautiful moments: a tranquil evening paddle on the lake, a hike through a stunning aspen forest, and a nap in my hammock, gently swaying between the trees. Come here mid-week with an open mind and a paddleboard and you might find serenity—and hopefully far fewer stinging insects!

O'Haver is located in one of my favorite parts of the state. Just north lies Salida, a charming town nestled in a river valley rubbing elbows with the jaw-dropping Collegiate Peaks to the west. O'Haver Lake Campground is just 25 minutes southwest of Salida, making it a nice place to camp if you fancy a day trip for ice cream or a dip in the mighty Arkansas River.

Yet the campground is a destination of its own. O'Haver Lake is the star and a prime place for fishing, canoeing, and bird-watching. Only nonmotorized watercraft are allowed, and stand-up paddleboarders are common here. There's an accessible fishing pier and three

Bluebird skies above O'Haver Lake

KEY INFORMATION

LOCATION: Salida

INFORMATION: U.S. Forest Service, Pike–San Isabel National Forests & Cimarron and Comanche National Grasslands, Salida Ranger District; 719-539-3591; fs.usda.gov/psicc

OPEN: Mid-May–mid-October

SITES: 32

EACH SITE HAS: Tent pad, fire ring, upright grill, picnic table

WHEELCHAIR ACCESS: An accessible fishing pier is located along the southwest side of the lake.

ASSIGNMENT: Some sites reservable at recreation.gov

REGISTRATION: On-site

AMENITIES: Vault toilets, trash service, water (during the season)

PARKING: At campsites only

FEE: $22 per night

ELEVATION: 9,200'

RESTRICTIONS:

PETS: Must be leashed

QUIET HOURS: 10 p.m.–6 a.m.

FIRES: In fire rings only

ALCOHOL: Permitted

VEHICLES: 45'

day-use parking areas. Thirty-two campsites wrap around the eastern edge of this 15-acre lake, all in varying proximity to the shoreline. Tall ponderosa pines interspersed with aspens provide a beautiful foreground for the 13,961-foot Mount Ouray in the distance. Three vault toilets and three drinking-water spigots service the campground, and trash collection is provided during the season. You can buy firewood on-site from the campground host in site 6.

Getting a site here can be tricky as the campground is growing in popularity. I love to nab a reservation when I can, especially for a weekend. You can always try for a first-come, first-served site. If you arrive midweek you should be able to get one. Sites 1–5, 7, 13, 21, 23, and 24 are first come, first served, while all other sites are reservable. Sites 18, 19, and 20 are some of the best for lake access (and for tent camping). The sites are large and well kept but quite close together, so they don't offer much privacy.

Considering how popular this place is, you might find yourself needing a little quietude. Here's a tip: walk past the last campsite on the west end of the lake and look for a gate. This leads to a walking trail, which loosely follows Grays Creek and eventually intersects with Marshall Pass Road. But you don't have to walk far to find yourself alongside an aspen forest, and before long the trail opens up to gorgeous views.

There's plenty of hiking and biking in the area as well. County Road 200/Marshall Pass Road, above O'Haver Lake, is a popular cycling route. Another option is the 11.5-mile Monarch Crest Trail. This is a very approachable section of the Continental Divide Trail from Monarch Pass to Marshall Pass, with incredible views of both sides of the Divide. It's also listed as one of the most popular mountain biking routes in the state—so if you're hiking, be prepared to step off the trail when you hear bikers approaching.

Shirley Site, located off US 285 and County Road 200 just below Poncha Pass, is a popular staging area for dirt bikes, ATVs, and mountain bikes during the summer months.

My recommendation? Get here midweek and settle in for a night or two to enjoy the lake, the views, and the gorgeous sunsets.

O'Haver Lake Campground

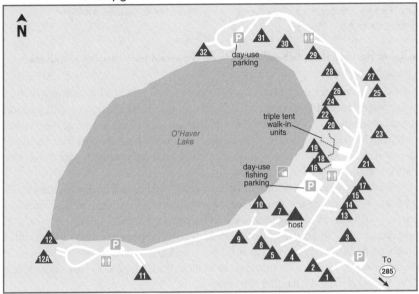

GETTING THERE

From Salida, travel west on US 50 to Poncha Springs. Turn south on US 285 and go 5 miles. Turn right and go west on CR 200 for 2.3 miles. Go west on CR 202 for 2.5 miles.

GPS COORDINATES: N38° 25.557' W106° 08.613'

A hiking trail near the campground

36

⛺Mueller State Park Campground

Beauty: ★★★★★ / Privacy: ★★★ / Spaciousness: ★★★ / Quiet: ★★★ / Security: ★★★★★ /
Cleanliness: ★★★★★

Mueller is the ideal place to break into Rocky Mountain tent camping and hiking.

For those who believe Rocky Mountain National Park to have the best scenery in the state, Mueller State Park will give you a run for your money. Mueller is blessed with a panoramic piece of land, with Pikes Peak in full view to the east and a long stretch of the Continental Divide in sight to the west. The spruce, fir, pine, and aspen trees, broken with meadows and rock outcrops, make up a canvas on which a clean, well-kept campground and a complete network of trails are beautifully painted.

Right away, campers will notice the commendable upkeep and quality facilities at Mueller State Park. While riding the smooth, paved road to the immaculate, well-groomed camping area, you'll wish all tenting locales could look this nice. Encompassing several different campgrounds, the camping area is set in the high country along Revenuers Ridge, with roads spurring off the main ridge road. The first spur road leads to Peak View Campground. Here, five campsites are set in woods that look up to Pikes Peak. These sites are usually dominated by RVs and are among the handful of campsites that are open year-round.

Gorgeous views from Turkey Meadow Walk-In Campground at Mueller State Park

KEY INFORMATION

LOCATION: Divide

INFORMATION: Colorado Parks & Wildlife, 719-687-2366, cpw.state.co.us

OPEN: Year-round (summer season: May 1–Sept. 30; winter season Oct. 1–April 30)

SITES: 136

EACH SITE HAS: Tent-only sites have tent pad, fire grate, picnic table; others also have water and electricity.

WHEELCHAIR ACCESS: Sites 12 and 22 are handicapped-designated sites; reserve by calling 800-244-5613 or at cpwshop.com.

ASSIGNMENT: By reservation only

REGISTRATION: 800-244-5613, cpwshop.com

AMENITIES: Hot showers, vault and flush toilets, laundry, phone

PARKING: At campsites or walk-in tent campers parking area

FEE: $9 Parks Pass, plus $28–36 per night

ELEVATION: 9,500'

RESTRICTIONS:

PETS: Must be leashed, not allowed on trails or in backcountry

QUIET HOURS: 10 p.m.–6 a.m.

FIRES: In fire grates only; not allowed in backcountry

ALCOHOL: Permitted

VEHICLES: 1 per site

OTHER: 14-day stay limit

The main campground road, divided into two one-way roads, has campsites all along it, including several pull-through sites. Then Conifer Ridge Campground splits off to the right. True to its name, spruce, fir, and pine cloak its slopes. All types of campers enjoy this area. Farther up on your left, past the Pisgah Point group campground, is Prospector Ridge Campground. Here, 12 walk-in sites make a prime location for tent campers. The woods are thick, and campsites are strung out far from one another for more than 100 yards. If you want the maximum in solitude and privacy, pitch your tent here.

More campsites are laid out along the main road as you continue to the 10-site Turkey Meadow Walk-In Campground. Pine and fir trees shade most of the sites, except those on the meadow's edge. No matter where you are, the view of Pikes Peak is majestic. Feel fortunate if you get one of these campsites. The camping area ends with more campsites and an auto turnaround on Grouse Mountain.

Though I thought that the walk-in tent campgrounds were the best, there is not a bad site in this well-designed campground. Water spigots and vault toilets are situated throughout Mueller. The showers, flush toilets, and laundry facilities are centrally located in the camper services building.

This campground stays booked from June through August. If you want to stay here—and I highly recommend that you do—try to come during the week. It is an ideal starter park for camping novices, and veterans will appreciate the extra special touches. There are also two equestrian campsites and three cabins available.

The trails here are similarly well marked and maintained. There are more than 44 miles of hiking trails and 36 miles of biking trails for recreationists of all skill levels. Some trails are also open to horseback riders. In the backcountry, you can hike to views, open meadows, and old homesteads and mines. There are several ponds in the backcountry to fish. Four-Mile Creek offers stream fishing for trout. You can even camp in the backcountry by hiking 1.25–1.5 miles from Black Bear Trailhead. These sites (1BC and 2BC) are each equipped with a tent pad and a bear box, and backcountry toilet facilities are available.

The south end of Mueller has the Four-Mile Day Use Area. This is the trailhead for the popular hike up to Dome Rock, which involves several creek crossings. You may see some bighorn sheep from this rock, which rises 800 feet above the valley below.

Park personnel can steer you in the right direction for a trail of your ability. Go to the visitor center for answers to questions and to check out the indoor wildlife habitat there. Rangers lead nature programs during the summer in this wildlife-rich park of 12,000 acres. Mueller State Park can get you on your way to being a Rocky Mountain hiking and camping pro.

While you are in the area, you may want to make a side trip to the historic mining towns of Cripple Creek and Victor. These communities have been revamped, offering a little history and a lot of gaming.

Mueller State Park Campground

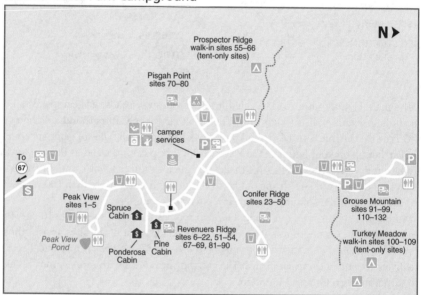

GETTING THERE

From Woodland Park, drive west on US 24 for 7 miles to Divide. Then turn left on CO 67 and go south 3.5 miles to Mueller State Park, which will be on your right.

GPS COORDINATES: N38° 52.779' W105° 10.863'

37

North Crestone Creek Campground

Beauty: ★★★★★ / Privacy: ★★★★★ / Spaciousness: ★★★ / Quiet: ★★★★ / Security: ★★★ /
Cleanliness: ★★★★

North Crestone offers creekside camping in a riparian forest perched against the Sangre de Cristo Mountains.

North Crestone Creek is one of the most charming campgrounds in southwestern Colorado. Here, along North Crestone Creek, there is an abundance of trees of various types, especially by Rocky Mountain standards; the campground's location in a forest transition zone along a well-watered valley produces this biodiversity. Cottonwoods, piñon pine, juniper, Douglas-fir, maple, alder, and aspen conspire to form a dense forest where campsites are nestled into nooks and crannies between streamside boulders.

North Crestone Creek crashes through the forest.

KEY INFORMATION

LOCATION: Crestone

INFORMATION: U.S. Forest Service,
Rio Grande National Forest; 719-655-2547;
fs.usda.gov/riogrande

OPEN: Mid-May–October

SITES: 13

EACH SITE HAS: Picnic table, fire ring,
bear box

WHEELCHAIR ACCESS: No designated
accessible sites

ASSIGNMENT: First come, first served;
no reservations

REGISTRATION: Self-registration on-site

AMENITIES: Vault toilets, trash collection;
no water

PARKING: At campsites only

FEE: $7 per night

ELEVATION: 8,300'

RESTRICTIONS:

PETS: Must be leashed

QUIET HOURS: None

FIRES: In fire grates only

ALCOHOL: At campsites only

VEHICLES: 25'

OTHER: 14-day stay limit

Its location in the foothills of the Sangre de Cristo Mountains is part of what makes this such a desirable place to tent camp—craggy, barren, snow-covered peaks; alpine lakes; and far-reaching views of the San Luis Valley and mountains beyond make the hiking here some of the most scenic in the state. The upper reaches of these highlands are protected wilderness.

The campground begins just after you enter the Rio Grande National Forest. You might see signs that say NORTH CRESTONE CAMPGROUND—don't worry, you're in the right place. On your left is a rocky, tree-studded canyon wall. To your right is the crashing Crestone Creek, shaded by all those wonderful trees. A heavy understory of younger trees and alders screens you from everyone else.

Almost all the campsites are set against the creek and count backwards from 13. Site 13 is home to the campground host, right across from a vault toilet. At each site, there is a picnic table, bear box, and fire grate. There are a couple of sites that offer some sun, but expect to be in the shade most of the time in this valley environment. Another set of toilets is across from site 5. The final two campsites are located just before the end of the road and trailhead parking. Site 2 is across the road from the creek—it's the only one that isn't directly next to North Crestone Creek. There is also a vault toilet up here. A vehicle turnaround and the mountains lie beyond the last campsites. You must bring your own water.

With so much beauty and so few sites, this is a popular weekend campground. The upside of having only 13 sites is that even when it's busy, it doesn't seem crowded. As with many first-come, first-served campsites, try getting here midweek to have your pick. Trying for a spot on a weekend might leave you disappointed. *Note:* If you come in early summer, bring the mosquito repellent . . . and the screen house, and the citronella, the whole nine yards. I came in early June and the little buggers were downright swarming.

The Sangre de Cristo Wilderness is just a walk away from your tent. The North Crestone Creek Trail leaves the upper end of the campground and connects to other trails in the wilderness, enabling trips to the high country. Venable Pass is 5 miles distant, as is North Crestone Lake. The trails are well marked and maintained. You can fish the creek or go all the way to North Crestone Lake, where the fishing is said to be good. Wildlife-viewing possibilities include seeing bighorn sheep and bears. Speaking of bears, they are known to slip into the campground during lean years, so use the provided bear boxes.

Campers sometimes walk the mile to the hamlet of Crestone to buy groceries or dine at one of the handful of restaurants. Unfortunately, the brewery closed in 2021. The living is nice and slow here, and the area is considered a spiritual center, with several world religions represented. While you are down there, check out a few more hiking opportunities. If you take the road past the post office and follow it 2 miles up, you will come to the Willow Lake Trailhead. South Crestone Trail climbs 4.5 miles to South Crestone Lake. There are several nice dispersed campsites along the route if you fancy an overnight. Willow Lake Trail leads 4.8 miles to Upper Willow Lake.

North Crestone Creek Campground

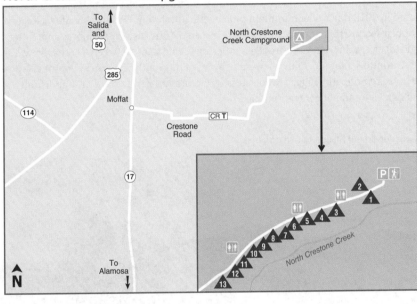

GETTING THERE

From Moffat, drive east on CR T (Crestone Road) 13 miles to the hamlet of Crestone. Veer left on Birch Street, then continue 1.2 miles as it winds through the town until you come to CR 71/Spillway Road. Turn left and follow this road to the campground.

GPS COORDINATES: N38° 00.788' W105° 41.642'

38

⚠ Trujillo Meadows Campground

Beauty: ★★★ / Privacy: ★★ / Spaciousness: ★★★★ / Quiet: ★★★ / Security: ★★★★ / Cleanliness: ★★★★

This is one of the more well-kept campgrounds in the Rio Grande National Forest, with much to see and do nearby.

Trujillo Meadows exudes a high-mountain aura from its perch near Cumbres Pass and the New Mexico state line. Open clearings of grass and cool breezes make summer wildflowers sway back and forth against the backdrop of the San Juan Mountains. The campground is spread wide over the montane setting, standing at over 10,000 feet. The altitude can delay the opening date due to snow, so call before you make the trek.

The 50-site getaway is an attractive spot, even though most of the trees in the area were cleared in 2012 due to the mountain pine beetle infestation. Trujillo Meadows Reservoir is a popular feature that anglers and canoers can enjoy. The historic Cumbres and Toltec Railroad still chugs through Cumbres Pass, offering scenic tours between Chama, New Mexico, and Antonito, Colorado. Only a few miles away, in the South San Juan Wilderness—possibly the most remote and rugged wilderness in Colorado—hikers have an opportunity to get back to a Colorado of generations past.

The road to Trujillo Meadows Campground

U.S. Forest Service

KEY INFORMATION

LOCATION: La Jara

INFORMATION: U.S. Forest Service,
Rio Grande National Forest; 719-852-5941;
fs.usda.gov/riogrande

OPEN: Memorial Day–Labor Day

SITES: 50

EACH SITE HAS: Picnic table, fire grate

WHEELCHAIR ACCESS: 1 ADA-compliant
site is available.

ASSIGNMENT: First come, first served;
no reservations

REGISTRATION: On-site

AMENITIES: Water, vault toilets, trash bins

PARKING: At campsites only

FEE: $26 per night

ELEVATION: 10,000'

RESTRICTIONS:

PETS: Must be leashed

QUIET HOURS: 10 p.m.–8 a.m.

FIRES: In fire grates only

ALCOHOL: At campsites only

VEHICLES: 40'

OTHER: 14-day stay limit

Leave the well-maintained Forest Service Road (FS) 118, and enter Trujillo Meadows. Pass the campground host, who is located at the entrance for your security and usually has firewood for sale. The rest of the sites on the upper and lower loops are fully exposed these days, after the beetle infestation forced the removal of the mature spruce forests. While this has taken away the once shady and private options for camping, having a sunny site may be a nice choice on cool, early-summer days. Today, native trees and newly planted saplings are filling in the void. For now, campers can enjoy expansive mountain vistas, as much of this campground is in open meadowland.

The lower loop is near a footpath to the parking area and boat launch for the Trujillo Meadows Reservoir. Across from campsites 40 and 41, there is an observation platform where campers and day-use visitors can view a waterfall. There are four vault toilets spread evenly throughout the campground, including one that was recently upgraded. Water and garbage bins are also available.

Forest Service personnel told me that, since the pandemic and wildfires struck elsewhere in Colorado, Trujillo Meadows has seen a resurgence in camping use. No matter the day or week, expect this campground to fill up. Try to get a spot midweek if you can; it's that popular. Bring all your supplies with you, as stores are scarce here in the South San Juan Wilderness.

Trujillo Meadows Reservoir lies just a short distance from the campground. Anglers can access walking trails to cast their lines for trout. If you bring a boat, keep your large motors home, as this reservoir is wakeless. A canoe, kayak, or paddleboard would be a better watercraft choice.

If Trujillo Meadows Campground is full when you arrive, try the 42-site Elk Creek Campground, located in the lower portion of the Conejos Canyon a short distance from Highway 17. Elk Creek flows adjacent to this campground, which is located at a slightly lower elevation of 8,500 feet and offers a mix of first-come, first-served and reservable campsites. Note that dispersed camping along FS 118 is prohibited.

For hikers, the South San Juan Wilderness is as wild as Colorado gets and has more than 180 miles of trails. This place is rugged. Hikers can pick up the Continental Divide Trail at

Cumbres Pass and head north into the South San Juan Wilderness. For an ideal day hike, find the Rio de Los Pinos Trailhead off FS 118, which gives access to the upper reaches of the Rio de Los Pinos, a popular fishing stream. This trail was recently rehabilitated for access by hikers and horses.

For a less sweaty way to see the scenery, take the Cumbres and Toltec Scenic Railroad. Ride in an open-air car pulled by a coal-burning locomotive, and get an eyeful of mountainous border country. It was originally built in 1880 to access the silver mining areas in southwestern Colorado's San Juan Mountains. The railroad is now listed on the National Register of Historic Places. So climb aboard, and let those old-timey engines do all the work.

Trujillo Meadows Campground

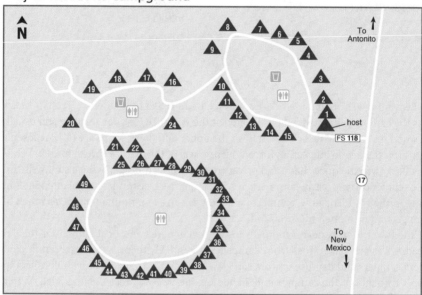

GETTING THERE

From the intersection of US 285 and CO 17 in Antonito, take CO 17 35.2 miles west to the Trujillo Meadows Reservoir sign. Turn right and go 0.1 mile to a T-intersection and campground sign. Turn right onto FS 118 and go 2.1 miles to the campground on your right.

GPS COORDINATES: N37° 02.805' W106° 26.917'

SOUTHWEST
COLORADO

View of the Gunnison River in Black Canyon of the Gunnison National Park (see page 134)

39

△ Black Canyon of the Gunnison National Park: North Rim Campground

Beauty: ★★★ / Privacy: ★★★ / Spaciousness: ★★★ / Quiet: ★★★★ / Security: ★★★★★ / Cleanliness: ★★★★

The Black Canyon of the Gunnison is a unique physical feature of Colorado and is a must-see for both locals and tourists. The North Rim Campground gives you front-row seats.

You won't believe how deep and narrow a gorge the Black Canyon is until you actually see it. As you drive toward the canyon rim, it seems to come out of nowhere, making it all the more jaw-dropping. There are many places to access the gorge, but the North Rim is the best for tent camping. It is the quietest and most primitive, set on the rim's edge in an ancient piñon/juniper forest. Instead of looking up at snowy mountains—your typical Colorado view—you will be looking down into a nearly 2,000-foot-deep canyon. You can hike along the rim or drop down into the gorge itself, where the fishing is great along a stretch of Colorado's Gold Medal Waters. Some of the best climbing in the state can be done here at "The Black," as it's known in the climbing world.

Make your drive from Crawford and slightly descend to the canyon along Grizzly Gulch. Pass the ranger station, and come to the North Rim Campground. Enter the loop and the piñon/juniper forest, which is complemented with Gambel oak and the bird-attracting

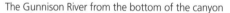

The Gunnison River from the bottom of the canyon

KEY INFORMATION

LOCATION: Gunnison

INFORMATION: National Park Service, 970-641-2337, nps.gov/blca

OPEN: Mid-May–mid-October

SITES: 13

EACH SITE HAS: Picnic table, fire grate, bear box

WHEELCHAIR ACCESS: No designated accessible sites

ASSIGNMENT: First come, first served

REGISTRATION: Self-registration on-site

AMENITIES: Water, vault toilet

PARKING: At campsites only

FEE: $16 per night; $30 park pass per vehicle

ELEVATION: 7,700'

RESTRICTIONS:

PETS: Must be leashed

QUIET HOURS: 10 p.m.–8 a.m.

FIRES: In fire grates only

ALCOHOL: At campsites only

VEHICLES: 22'

OTHER: 14-day stay limit

serviceberry. As you look for a campsite, note the gnarled trees here. Some are more than 700 years old! It is a rare opportunity indeed to camp among such ancient trees. Trailers are limited to 22 feet.

The campground lies on a fair slope heading down toward the canyon. The smaller gorge of SOB Draw (which is short for what you think it is) wraps around the campground. Campsites are on both sides of the road beneath the old trees, which offer the ideal amount of sun and shade. The understory is primarily dirt, which can make for a dusty campsite. Overall, the campsites are on the small side, which discourages nearly all but tent campers, especially after big-rig drivers see how the old trees crowd the road; they just turn right around. A vault toilet and water spigot are in the center of the small campground. Be advised that the water may not be turned on early or late in the camping season. There's no electricity, no firewood, and no cell reception.

At the end of the loop is the Chasm View Nature Trail, which truly delivers. The view into the gorge is breathtaking. You can just make out the roar of the Gunnison River far below. There are old trees on the Chasm View Trail, too. The North Vista Trail leaves from the ranger station. The path goes along the North Rim of the Gunnison to a high point on a nearby ridge. But the highlight is the side trip to Exclamation Point. Some of the best views of the inner canyon are found here.

So you want to make the challenging descent to, and the more challenging ascent from, the canyon floor? There are three ways in from the North Rim. The SOB Draw Route starts near the campground. It is 2 hours down and 3 hours up the 2-mile route, which includes several 8- to 12-foot ledges to climb. Watch for the poison ivy growing thick along the way. Long Draw is a mile-long drop that starts near the Balanced Rock Overlook; beware of poison ivy growing 5 feet high here. Slide Draw is very steep and starts near the Kneeling Camel View. Anglers in search of the big trout can brave the poison ivy and test the lesser-fished waters. *Note:* These trails are wilderness routes and are not maintained. They are essentially unmarked scrambles to the river and are only for those who are in excellent physical condition and who come prepared. These routes are high-risk; the park recommends that hikers be prepared for self-rescue. Did I mention the poison ivy? There are a few campsites along each of the routes; all climbers and backcountry visitors must obtain a free backcountry permit at the ranger station.

For views from the road, simply exit the campground and drive along the gravel rim road. Be very careful—the views are quite distracting. At the end of this road is the Deadhorse Trail. This 2.5-mile path traces an old road with views into Deadhorse Gulch and the main canyon.

If you happen to be looking for camping outside the summer season or want to see Black Canyon of the Gunnison from another perspective, the South Rim is your destination. The campground there doesn't offer the proximity, views, or quietude of the North Rim, but it's open all year, it's exceptionally well-maintained, and it still has plenty of access to views and trails from the opposite side of the canyon. I especially enjoyed the Warner Point Nature Trail, which begins at the far end of Rim Drive Road. Pick up a trail guide at the High Point Overlook and follow a preservationist's journey through serviceberry, piñon pine, and juniper, with incredible views of the San Juan Mountain Range, Uncompahgre Valley, West Elk Mountains, and, of course, the Black Canyon itself.

Black Canyon of the Gunnison National Park: North Rim Campground

GETTING THERE

From Crawford, drive south on CO 92 for 3 miles to Black Canyon Road. Turn right on Black Canyon Road and follow it as it twists and turns through the countryside for 4 miles. Turn right to stay on Black Canyon Road. In 0.8 mile, turn left to stay on Black Canyon Road. In 1.9 mile, veer right to stay on Black Canyon Road. In 5 miles, veer right, following signs for the ranger station. The campground is 0.8 mile ahead, past the station.

GPS COORDINATES: N38° 35.114' W107° 42.600'

40

Burro Bridge Campground

Beauty: ★★★★ / Privacy: ★★★★ / Spaciousness: ★★★★ / Quiet: ★★★★★ / Security: ★★★ / Cleanliness: ★★★★

Burro Bridge is a tent camping gem near the Lizard Head Wilderness, home to the high peaks of the San Miguel Mountains.

If you're looking for a remote retreat into nature, Burro Bridge is it. The site of the small campground is the head of a meadow, fringed in woodland on a perch above the West Dolores River. It meets the expectations of high-country beauty you've come to expect in Colorado's national forest campgrounds. The nearby Lizard Head Wilderness may be one of the state's most beautiful wildlife areas, with 37 miles of wilderness playground for experienced hikers and climbers. Proximity to this wilderness makes Burro Bridge a tent camper's choice campground. Those with horses are welcome here too.

The 14 campsites are strung along a two-way gravel road with a vehicle turnaround at the end. Aspen and spruce are the primary forest components. The understory is grass, flowers, and young aspens. To your left as you drive in are the meadow and a rising mountain of solid aspens. To your right is the small canyon of the West Dolores River. An attractive log fence borders the campground along the edge of the precipice that drops down into the West Dolores River.

Gazing into the woods from Burro Bridge Campground

Jason Stockbridge

KEY INFORMATION

LOCATION: Dolores

INFORMATION: U.S. Forest Service, San Juan National Forest, Dolores Ranger District; 970-882-7296; fs.usda.gov/sanjuan

OPEN: Mid-May–October

SITES: 14

EACH SITE HAS: Picnic table, fire ring

WHEELCHAIR ACCESS: 1 campsite has a table suitable for wheelchairs.

ASSIGNMENT: First come, first served; no reservations

REGISTRATION: On-site (self-registration, or register with camp host)

AMENITIES: Water pump, vault toilets, horse corral with 2 bays

PARKING: At campsites only

FEE: $22 per night

ELEVATION: 9,000'

RESTRICTIONS:

PETS: Must be leashed

QUIET HOURS: 10 p.m.–6 p.m.

FIRES: In fire rings only

ALCOHOL: At campsites only

VEHICLES: 35'

OTHER: 14-day stay limit

The first campsite is nestled in a shade-lending spruce coppice. The next two are by the canyon but are more open, and each has a shade tree near the picnic table. Farther down, a few sites are away from the river in a sunny meadow. The camp host told me that these are often used for campers with horses. They have little shade but good views of the surrounding mountains.

The road climbs gently up along the meadow, passing the vault toilets and a pump well. Campsites continue on the right, with plenty of shade. Site 11 is the most private, at the end of the loop, and site 12 is the most exposed, surrounded by young aspens in the middle of the vehicle turnaround. Overall, the large distance between campsites makes privacy less of an issue and spaciousness the norm.

With so many campgrounds in the area and being farther from the main roads, Burro Bridge receives light use. On the way here, you'll pass Mavreeso Campground and West Dolores Campground—both nice alternatives but definitely more crowded. On the other hand, you may have Burro Bridge all to yourself on a weekday, like my family and I did. Weekends may see a few other tent and horse campers, but expect to find a campsite on all but the major summer holidays. Be bear-aware, and be sure to safely stash your trash as there are no trash services here; the campground host told me that bears frequent this campground each summer.

Though it is not the highest peak, the 400-foot spire at its top makes Lizard Head the most conspicuous mountain in the wilderness. Only expert climbers attempt to scale this monolith. There are three fourteeners (14,000' or higher mountains) in the Lizard Head Wilderness (Wilson Peak, Mount Wilson, and El Diente). Alpine lakes, waterfalls, and deserted mines complement the high mountains.

Your ticket to all this is the Navajo Lake Trail (#635), which starts a mile above Burro Bridge. The 7.3-mile trail begins at Forest Service Road (FS) 535 and is open to hikers and horses. Much of this hiking will be at or above timberline, so bring clothing for changes in weather. A good loop hike would be to take Burro Bridge Trail from the campground to Groundhog Stock Drive Trail to connect with Navajo Lake Trail. Turn right on the

Kilpacker Trail and loop back to the Groundhog Stock Drive Trail; then follow the forest road above Burro Bridge back to the campground.

A good view of the peaks of Lizard Head can be seen while driving over CO 145 to Lizard Head Pass, through which the historic Rio Grande Southern Railroad once wound. Start a high-country hike from Lizard Head Pass to the spire of Lizard Head on the Lizard Head Trail.

The Calico Trail is also near Burro Bridge. Use FS 471, then make this 17-mile network of trails any length you like. Mountain bikers should take note of the Stoner Mesa area. This and the Taylor Mesa area offer 150 square miles of high-country forest for hikers, bikers, equestrians, and four-wheel-drive vehicles. Set up camp at Burro Bridge, get out your San Juan National Forest map, and begin exploring.

Burro Bridge Campground

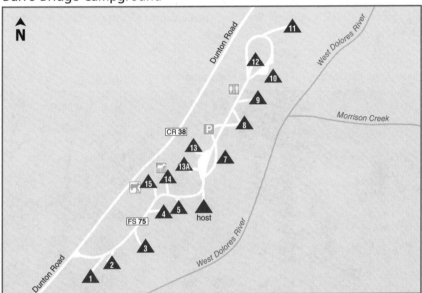

GETTING THERE

From Dolores, drive north on CO 145 for 13 miles, then turn left on CR 38 (West Dolores Road). Follow CR 38 for 25 miles on a well-maintained dirt road to Burro Bridge Campground, which will be on your right.

GPS COORDINATES: N37° 47.105' W108° 03.933'

41

Cathedral Campground

Beauty: ★★★★ / Privacy: ★★★ / Spaciousness: ★★★ / Quiet: ★★★★ / Security: ★★ / Cleanliness: ★★★

The camping here is free, quiet, and relaxed.

Getting to Cathedral Campground from South Fork requires a quick turn off speedy US 160. From there, the road gets quiet and turns into a single-lane washboard for 7 miles until you pull into the campground.

You'll notice right away that the U.S. Forest Service doesn't charge you to camp here. It's rare that you have the opportunity to camp without shelling out bucks just for a spot to pitch your tent. While they aren't immaculately maintained, there are plenty of good campsites in this campground. Many are set in a mixed forest of aspen and blue spruce right along Embargo Creek. Cathedral Rock and the La Garita Mountains loom over the locale from across the creek.

Embargo Creek babbles through Cathedral Campground.

KEY INFORMATION

LOCATION: Del Norte

INFORMATION: U.S. Forest Service, Rio Grande National Forest; 719-657-3321; fs.usda.gov/riogrande

OPEN: Year-round (may be inaccessible in winter)

SITES: 22

EACH SITE HAS: Picnic table, fire grate

WHEELCHAIR ACCESS: No designated accessible sites

ASSIGNMENT: First come, first served; no reservations

REGISTRATION: Not needed

AMENITIES: Vault toilets; no water

PARKING: At campsites only

FEE: None

ELEVATION: 9,400'

RESTRICTIONS:

PETS: Must be leashed

QUIET HOURS: None

FIRES: In fire grates only

ALCOHOL: At campsites only

VEHICLES: 35'

OTHER: 14-day stay limit

The 22 campsites are split about evenly on two loops. The upper loop is higher up along the creek. In fact, the upper part of this loop lies astride the confluence of Embargo and Cathedral Creeks. A small clearing lies in the lower center of the loop, as campsites are strung along the heavily wooded banks of Embargo Creek. The forest here is so dense that many of the campsites receive very little sunlight. Others are more open as the loop enters a pocket of old aspens. Then the loop turns back downstream and comes to the clearing again. Each loop has a vault toilet.

The lower loop drops down along Embargo Creek. The woods are denser throughout this loop with very few sunny sites. Judging by the vegetation growing on some of the vehicle pull-in areas on the upper part of the loop, these sites receive very little use. The lower sites along the creek get taken first.

This place is a sweet slice of forest in which to relax and escape the trials of modern life. Cathedral is rarely more than half full—usually less than that—and it is very quiet. The woods provide ample privacy, and the sites are average in size. It feels a bit worn-in, without the bells and whistles of high-amenity campgrounds. But for some, that's just the ticket to a relaxing night or two in nature.

Truly, relaxing and getting away from it all are at the top of the list here. But if you get tent fever, there are some good hiking trails that leave right from the campground, and other trails are nearby. Cathedral Creek Trail starts near campsite 9 and leads up Cathedral Creek for almost 4 miles to Cathedral Rock. In early summer, wildflowers line the trail. You'll make many crossings of the creek, eventually passing a waterfall on the way up to the jagged cliffs of Cathedral Rock.

Farther up Forest Service Road (FS) 640 you can find Embargo Trailhead, from which you can hike more than 6 miles toward Mesa Mountain along Embargo Creek. Views open up a few miles from the campground. Fremont Camp Trail starts up FS 640 a short distance above the campground. Here is where explorer John Fremont and his men spent a long and deadly winter.

Both Cathedral and Embargo Creeks offer excellent trout fishing near the campground. Fly-fishing is easier below the campground in the lower elevations along Embargo Creek, where the forest is more open. But if you want to go for the big ones, head down to the Rio Grande. Many portions of the river are Colorado gold-medal fishing waters (catch-and-release areas that allow the trout to grow larger). Rafting is also a popular way to enjoy the Rio Grande. The rapids are generally Class II and III. Outfitters are stationed in both South Fork and Del Norte.

Cathedral Campground

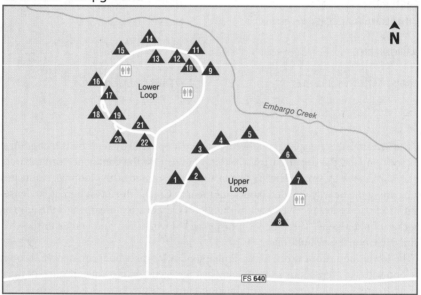

GETTING THERE

From Del Norte, head west on US 160 for 9 miles to Embargo Creek Road. Turn right on Embargo Creek Road and follow the signs for Cathedral Campground 15 miles distant on FS 650 then FS 640. Cathedral Campground will be on your right.

GPS COORDINATES: N37° 49.402' W106° 36.267'

42

⛺ Lost Lake Campground

Beauty: ★★★★★ / Privacy: ★★★ / Spaciousness: ★★★ / Quiet: ★★★★ / Security: ★★★ / Cleanliness: ★★★

Come to Lost Lake and find your happy place. This family-friendly spot has it all: inspiring views, leisurely hikes, and good fishing.

The setting at Lost Lake Campground is classic. A shimmering jewel of water is perched high in the mountains with a forested backdrop from which snowy, granite twin peaks rise majestically. Most of the campsites have views of this inspiring sight, as if the Kebler Pass Road wasn't scenic enough on the way up. Rising out of the West Elk Wilderness, East and West Beckwith Mountains form twin sentinels over Lost Lake Slough, the body of water beside which you camp. (The actual Lost Lake is farther up in the mountains, less than a mile distant.)

Not only do you have some of the most scenic tent camping in Colorado, but you are also within a mile of two wilderness areas: the West Elk Wilderness and the Raggeds Wilderness to the north, home to those pointed peaks you saw off to your left as you drove up. So if you get bored with relaxing and fishing at Lost Lake, there are nearly 300 miles of trails between the two wilderness areas on which you can exhaust yourself.

Epic scenery at Lost Lake Campground

Dan Collier/Shutterstock

KEY INFORMATION

LOCATION: Paonia

INFORMATION: U.S. Forest Service; Grand Mesa, Uncompahgre, and Gunnison National Forests; Paonia Ranger District; 970-527-4131; fs.usda.gov/gmug

OPEN: June 18–Oct. 5

SITES: 19 (including 5 equestrian sites not shown on map)

EACH SITE HAS: Picnic table, fire grate

WHEELCHAIR ACCESS: Accessible day-use picnic area and fishing platform along the north side of Lost Lake Slough

ASSIGNMENT: First come, first served; no reservations

REGISTRATION: Not needed

AMENITIES: Vault toilet, water, fishing access

PARKING: At campsites and at picnic area (for a fee)

FEE: $20 per night

ELEVATION: 9,600'

RESTRICTIONS:

PETS: Must be leashed

QUIET HOURS: 10 p.m.–8 a.m.

FIRES: In fire grates only

ALCOHOL: At campsites only

VEHICLES: 60'

OTHER: 14-day stay limit. Campers must store food and other items in a hard-sided vehicle or other bearproof container.

When you finally make it to Lost Lake Slough, veer left to the east spur route. There's a host site at the entrance to this spur. The main drive runs along the lake. Among the campsite options are four pull-through sites, four double sites, and two sites right on the lake. Farther down, an additional five campsites lie on the west loop; these sites cater more to RVs due to their average spur of 60 feet. Smaller RVs are advisable, as there are no hookups.

Lost Lake is impeccably maintained, with a friendly camp host to help you find the best available campsite when you arrive. Improvements from 2011 still hold up today, with level tent pads, updated picnic tables, fire rings, vault toilets, dumpsters, and a potable-water system as well as improved roads and better signage.

As always, call ahead before making the long drive to camp here (or anywhere) in case of unpredictable weather. Campground access is dependent on the snow; the Forest Service will open it as soon as the road is open. The campground may be a gem, but it's no longer hidden; a Forest Service rep told me it fills up every single summer afternoon.

In the summer, wildflowers abound. In fall, golden aspens dance on the glassy water's edge. The prominent spires of the Ruby Range give the Raggeds Wilderness its name. Aspens and conifers grace the lower, wooded slopes. Trails lead into this land off Kebler Pass Road, both before and after the turnoff to Lost Lake Campground. On your way up, you passed the trailhead for Trail 836, which leads down Trout Creek. To enjoy the higher alpine country, drive toward Kebler Pass and head north on Trail 830, which passes a few lakes as it parallels the Ruby Range.

A short walk away from the campgrounds is the Beckwith Pass Trail, which heads south into the 17,600-acre West Elk Wilderness. Your hike leads south to Beckwith Pass, which isn't usually passable until mid-July. It's a little more than 2 miles to the pass. From there, you can split left to the Cliff Creek Trail, which is actually just before the pass, or continue into the heart of the West Elk. Allow yourself ample time to return before dark.

Closer to home is Three Lakes Trail, which departs from the campground. It offers a 3-mile loop hike that extends to the timber line and passes the actual Lost Lake and Dollar Lake. You'll see plenty of vibrant wildflowers in the summer, as well as a waterfall and three pristine lakes. The fishing right at Lost Lake Slough is a great choice, though, as it's periodically restocked. You can either bank fish or get onto the lake in any hand-propelled craft.

Lost Lake Campground

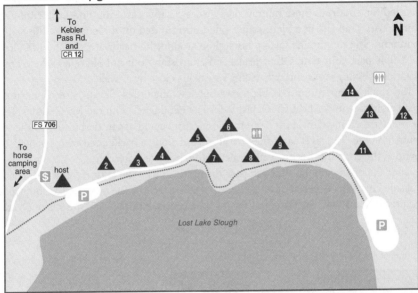

GETTING THERE

From Paonia, drive north on CO 133 for 15 miles to CR 12 (Kebler Pass Road). The sign at the right turn will say CRESTED BUTTE. Turn right on Kebler Pass Road and follow it 14.5 miles. Turn right on Forest Service Road 706 and drive 2 more miles to Lost Lake Campground.

GPS COORDINATES: N38° 52.163' W107° 12.550'

⛺ Lost Trail Campground

Beauty: ★★★★ / Privacy: ★★★ / Spaciousness: ★★★ / Quiet: ★★★★ / Security: ★★ / Cleanliness: ★★★

Splendid isolation is found at Lost Trail.

Sometimes a long drive on a dirt road ends in disappointment. Other times, you are rewarded for enduring those bumpy, dusty rides. In this case, you find Lost Trail Campground. Lost Trail sits in a picturesque valley surrounded on three sides by the San Juan Mountains. The mountains form a horseshoe around the headwaters of the Rio Grande, which flow past your tent. Other peaks and crags stand out in bold relief. There are two outstanding hiking areas and two fishing reservoirs close by as well.

The small campground has big views but few amenities. Seven basic campsites are spread alongside lower Lost Creek just before its confluence with the Rio Grande. Nestled in a rock-strewn meadow, Lost Trail has some spruce and aspen that testify to the tough winters up here. The level campsites are all spread along a rocky road with a vehicle turnaround at the end. There is one vault toilet but no potable water.

Enter the open campground and pass the first campsite on your right, which lies right alongside Lost Trail Creek and has the shade of some spruce. The next site has some mature aspen trees that shade the table, but most of the spur sits in the sun. Site 3 is opposite the

This remote spot offers sparse shade but great views, with fishing and several hiking trails nearby.

U.S. Forest Service

KEY INFORMATION

LOCATION: Creede

INFORMATION: U.S. Forest Service, Rio Grande National Forest, Divide Ranger District; 719-658-2556; fs.usda.gov/riogrande

OPEN: Year-round; may be inaccessible due to snow or road closures November–mid-May

SITES: 7

EACH SITE HAS: Picnic table, fire ring

WHEELCHAIR ACCESS: No designated accessible sites

ASSIGNMENT: First come, first served; no reservations

REGISTRATION: Not needed

AMENITIES: Vault toilet; no water or trash collection

PARKING: At campsites only

FEE: None

ELEVATION: 9,600'

RESTRICTIONS:

PETS: Must be leashed

QUIET HOURS: 10 p.m.–8 a.m.

FIRES: In fire rings only

ALCOHOL: At campsites only

VEHICLES: 25'

OTHER: 14-day stay limit

---

creek and has a pull-through gravel pad. The views are outstanding, but the shade is lacking as it sits in an open meadow. Site 4 is similar, with a dead-end spur.

The fifth site is down along the creek far away from the others. A mature spruce tree at the end of the spur provides a little shade for the table. The sixth site is on a rocky knoll in the center of the turnaround. A few aspens offer scant shade. The last site is away from the creek in the meadow, with scattered spruce and minimal shade.

These sites feel fairly exposed, but don't worry too much about privacy—most people who drive this far are going to be like-minded tent campers who want to get way off the beaten track. Despite its distance from civilization, this campground does get busy in the summer months.

If you tire of the view from the campground, take a hike. The trail system around here is outstanding. The Lost Creek Trailhead is just a bit up the road. Here you can take the Lost Creek Trail up to Heart Lake or go toward the old mining area up toward the Continental Divide. About 30 minutes up the Lost Creek Trail, you'll find yourself at the junction with the West Lost Creek Trail. Turn left here and come to a giant landslide caused by avalanche activity in 1991. A lake was formed from this event, and the U.S. Forest Service has stocked it.

The Continental Divide Trail is almost 15 miles west on Forest Service Road (FS) 520 near Stony Pass. This is the easy way to see the high country. The old Beartown mining site is off FS 520 on FS 506. Just down from the campground is the Ute Creek Trailhead. After fording the Rio Grande, you can access the Weminuche Wilderness along Ute Creek. This makes for an isolated fishing experience. Avoid trespassing on the private footbridge on the Sky Hi Ranch.

Two nearby reservoirs also offer fishing. Rio Grande Reservoir is closer, but it's harder to fish on unless you have a boat. It has more than 1,200 surface acres of trout water. Road Canyon Reservoir is about 12.5 miles east, on the road back to Creede, but is much better suited for bank fishing. It has only 140 surface acres, but the shoreline has a gentle grade, parking areas, and spots to put a chair. The fishing is said to be good.

Bring everything you need with you to Lost Trail Campground. Supplies are limited in Creede, and you don't want to make an extra trip down that bumpy gravel road.

Lost Trail Campground

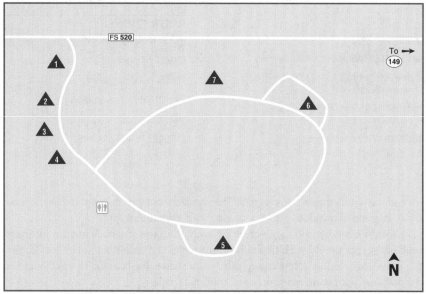

GETTING THERE

From Creede, head west on CO 149 for 20 miles to FS 520 (Rio Grande Reservoir Road) and turn left. Follow FS 520 for 18 miles to Lost Trail Campground, which will be on your left.

GPS COORDINATES: N37° 46.100' W107° 20.950'

44

⛺ Mesa Verde National Park: Morefield Campground

Beauty: ★★★ / Privacy: ★★ / Spaciousness: ★★★ / Quiet: ★★★ / Security: ★★★★★ / Cleanliness: ★★★★★

Camp at the largest campground in the national park system to see the famous cliff dwellings and more at Mesa Verde.

I was concerned that Mesa Verde was overrated, but it's a must see! Witnessing the preserved remains of an ancient culture, along with the area's inherent beauty, is one of Colorado's finest natural experiences. While driving on the park entrance road it all starts to sink in: cliff dwellings and ancient communities, the Mancos Valley and San Juan scenery—this place is special.

The most extraordinary trait of Morefield Campground is its size: 267 campsites. It is a pleasant enough place to stay and has adequate amenities to keep you from leaving the mesa, but the park itself is the reason you come here. From the ranger-led tours to the view-laden hiking to the good auto touring to the high-quality ranger programs every night, Mesa Verde National Park has more than enough attractions to make you want to stay longer.

Most of the campsites at Morefield are divided into eight loops and are spread out in a basin surrounded by ridges of trees and stone. In the basin, the primary vegetation is bushy

The ancient cliff dwellings are the main attraction at Mesa Verde National Park.

KEY INFORMATION

LOCATION: Cortez

INFORMATION: National Park Service, 970-564-4300, nps.gov/meve; Aramark, 800-449-2288, visitmesaverde.com

OPEN: Mid-April–October

SITES: 267, some group sites

EACH SITE HAS: Picnic table, fire grate, tent pads

WHEELCHAIR ACCESS: Accessible campsites and restrooms available in Apache Loop

ASSIGNMENT: First come, first served and by reservation

REGISTRATION: At campground entry station, 800-449-2288, visitmesaverde.com

AMENITIES: Water, flush toilets, community dish sinks, phone, showers, laundry, campground store and café, kennel

PARKING: At campsites only

FEE: $36 per night for tent sites, $50 per night for full hook-up RV sites, plus $20–$30 park entrance fee, depending on season; extra charge for more than 2 people (age 6 or older) per site

ELEVATION: 8,100'

RESTRICTIONS:

PETS: Must be leashed; not allowed on trails, in archaeological sites, or in buildings; kennel requires proof of vaccination

QUIET HOURS: 10 p.m.–6 a.m.

FIRES: In fire grates only

ALCOHOL: At campsites only

VEHICLES: 46'; limit of 2 per site

OTHER: 14-day stay limit

Gambel oak with some occasional piñon pine. Each loop has clean comfort stations with flush toilets and combination water fountains/spigots, and some with a community sink area.

Pay your fee at the campground entry station. Reservations are accepted but are not required, and either way you won't choose your exact campsite until you arrive. Tent campers share Morefield Campground evenly with RV and pop-up campers, so prepare for a busier, louder experience, especially in summer.

Campsite spaciousness is average; privacy depends on the amount of tree cover, which varies considerably. The forest's understory is generally grassy, with some sections of sage and brush. Jemez Loop is popular with tent campers. Down the way, Pueblo Road leads to three loops and lots of campsites. This area is on a hill and has some piñon pines. The Zuni Loop is one of the better locations and has many good tent sites with a variety of sun and shade. There are good views from here across the basin of Prater Ridge.

Stay away from the Ute Loop. It is the only loop with hookups and is the place of choice for RV campers. The Oraibi, Walpi, and Hano loops are all connected to one another. This area has many campsites that take a beating from the sun. The far views are good, but the near views of your fellow campers can be a little too close. My family and I stayed in the Apache Loop, which is sometimes closed until the campground begins to fill up, and it was nice to be a bit on the outskirts.

Showers are free for campers, and laundry is available for a small price. There is also a camp store, gift shop, café, and gas station. Snack bars are located at Chapin and Wetherill Mesas. Far View Lodge, located within the park, offers fine dining. You really can have it all!

Now, the reason you came: to see the cliff dwellings. You must buy a ticket to go on a ranger-led tour of the three primary dwellings: Long House, Cliff Palace, and Balcony House. Each one was constructed in the 1200s by the Ancestral Puebloans who made their lives atop the "Green Table." Cliff Palace has more than 150 rooms. The ranger leading the tours will satisfy your curiosity about each of the sites. You may be able to tour the Spruce Tree House on your own.

Be sure to check the national park website before you go, as many of the sites were closed during our visit. If they are running, book an all-day or half-day concessionaire guided tour of the park; these depart from Far View Lodge and Morefield Campground every morning. Mesa Verde is one place where it is smart to be led around by an expert. You'll likely have many questions, and these rangers have answers.

After setting up camp, check out the park's visitor center and museum to get oriented. You'll come to the campground miles before the visitor center and museum. Make the Chapin Mesa driving tour and see the pit houses that came before the cliff dwellings. View other cliff dwellings from the road. The views of the landscape are exciting too. If you download the NPS app, you can access a very good audio tour as you drive from site to site.

Return to the campground to make the 1.5-mile walk out the Knife Edge to watch the sunset. And for the next day, there is Wetherill Mesa, Prater Ridge, the Cedar Tree Tower, and . . . this place will keep you busy.

Mesa Verde National Park: Morefield Campground

GETTING THERE

From Cortez drive east on US 160 for 7.5 miles. Turn right onto Mesa Verde Ruins Road, and drive 4 miles to Morefield Campground, on your right.

GPS COORDINATES: N37° 11.267' W108° 29.233'

45

⛺ Mirror Lake Campground

Beauty: ★★★★ / Privacy: ★★★ / Spaciousness: ★★★ / Quiet: ★★★★ / Security: ★★★ / Cleanliness: ★★★

Mirror Lake Campground offers a restful alpine setting for tent campers who want to escape the summer heat.

Perched on the western edge of the Continental Divide, Mirror Lake reflects the granite Rocky Mountains rimmed in verdant forests that colorfully contrast with the Colorado blue sky. Here you can come to escape the stress of modern civilization and reflect on the restorative qualities that a day, a week, or a weekend in our grand national forests can have on your attitude. Though the amenities here are minimal, the perk of easy access to a mountain lake right on the divide is especially attractive.

While climbing sharply in your car along East Willow Creek, appreciate not only the beauty of the region but also the fact that you can access this high lake without having to backpack in with all your supplies. This same high elevation that lends such beauty also keeps campers from wandering up here in June, when the campground may or may not be open. Call ahead before you make the drive. The rough road and 16-foot vehicle length limit also deters nearly all folks except determined tent campers. Mirror Lake does get some weekend business, especially later in the summer.

Mirror Lake Campground offers several sites right on the 27-acre, clear-water lake.

U.S. Forest Service

KEY INFORMATION

LOCATION: Gunnison

INFORMATION: U.S. Forest Service; Grand Mesa, Uncompahgre, and Gunnison National Forests; 970-641-0471; fs.usda.gov/gmug

OPEN: Early June–late September

SITES: 10

EACH SITE HAS: Picnic table, fire ring

WHEELCHAIR ACCESS: No designated accessible campsites

ASSIGNMENT: First come, first served; no reservations

REGISTRATION: Self-registration on-site

AMENITIES: Vault toilet; no water

PARKING: At campsites only

FEE: $12 per night

ELEVATION: 11,000'

RESTRICTIONS:

PETS: Must be leashed

QUIET HOURS: None

FIRES: In fire rings only

ALCOHOL: Permitted

VEHICLES: 16'

OTHER: 14-day stay limit

The road becomes very steep just before arriving at the lake. Make the right turn into the campground and climb another hill. Campsites appear to the left in a stand of spruce, hidden from the water. Then you pop out on a small hill and the lake comes into view. On a calm day, it lives up to its name, reflecting Fitzpatrick Peak, Tincup Pass, and Emma Burr Mountain. Lakeside camping is a real treat, and Mirror Lake Campground offers several campsites right on the water—albeit a bit sun-drenched. A big windstorm a few years back resulted in several downed trees.

If you continue straight instead of turning right into the campground, you will come to the boat launch and parking area. The road that traces the east bank of the lake is the rough, four-wheel-drive road over 12,154-foot-high Tincup Pass, which continues to the ghost town of St. Elmo and, eventually, Mount Princeton Hot Springs Resort. To maintain a peaceful atmosphere, only hand-propelled craft are allowed on Mirror Lake. Mirror Lake encompasses 27 acres of clear water that harbors brook and rainbow trout. Forty percent of the bank is fishable; if you bring a kayak or canoe, you can get to that other 60% of shoreline that everyone else misses.

Stream fishers can follow the outlet of Mirror Lake, East Willow Creek, where you can catch rainbow, brown, brook, or cutthroat trout. And if you follow East Willow Creek down, you'll come to the big water (and big fish) of Taylor Reservoir. The 2,000-acre lake offers the four fish species described above, plus kokanee salmon, lake trout, and pike. There are boat ramps here as well.

If you don't feel like fishing, take a walk. The four-wheel-drive road up to Tincup Pass is a couple of miles to the top and makes a great day hike. If you prefer, tramp a section of the Timberline Trail. The trailhead is a few hundred yards below the campground. This path generally follows the timberline north below the Sawatch Range. You can take the trail just a mile or so to Garden Basin and an old mine site, or you can walk all the way to Sanford Creek.

If you need some time for reflection in a gorgeous high alpine setting, Mirror Lake may be one of your best options.

Mirror Lake Campground

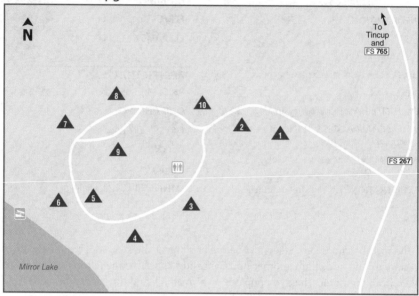

GETTING THERE

From Almont, drive north on Forest Service Road 742 (Taylor Canyon Road) for 22 miles to Taylor Park Reservoir. Turn right at the sign for Tincup onto FS 765, and follow FS 765 for 8 miles to Tincup. In Tincup, turn left on FS 267 and follow it 3 miles to Mirror Lake Campground, on the right.

GPS COORDINATES: N38° 44.850' W106° 25.917'

46

Ridgway State Park Campgrounds

Beauty: ★★★★★ / Privacy: ★★★ / Spaciousness: ★★★★ / Quiet: ★★★★ / Security: ★★★★★ /
Cleanliness: ★★★★★

This is one of the finest state parks in Colorado, if not the country.

One of the newer Colorado state parks, Ridgway is centered around a 1,000-surface-acre reservoir once known as the Dallas Creek Project, completed by the Bureau of Reclamation in 1987. This well-designed recreational area expertly integrates park facilities with the natural features of the land. Three high-quality campgrounds with two walk-in tent camping areas and plenty of amenities make this a must-stop for all campers. Twenty RV sites and 15 walk-in tent sites are open year-round, and everything is open from April through October. Three yurts are also available year-round.

The 300-acre Dutch Charlie area features two campgrounds: Dakota Terraces Campground and Elk Ridge Campground. The Dakota Terraces Campground is on lower, open terrain by the lake and has electrical hook-ups, meaning it's attractive to RVs. Instead, consider pitching your tent at the Elk Ridge Campground, high above the lake in a piñon/juniper forest. Walk through the trees for views of the San Juan and Cimarron mountain

Elk Ridge Campground overlooks Ridgway Reservoir.

KEY INFORMATION

LOCATION: Ridgway

INFORMATION: Colorado Parks & Wildlife; 970-626-5822, ext. 10; cpw.state.co.us

OPEN: Year-round

SITES: 25 walk-in, tent-only sites; 258 other

EACH SITE HAS: Tent-only sites have tent pad, fire grate, grill, picnic table; others also have water and electricity.

WHEELCHAIR ACCESS: All restroom and shower buildings are accessible; campsites 46, 105, 107, 230, 280, and 281 are suggested for disabled visitors.

ASSIGNMENT: By reservation only

REGISTRATION: 800-244-5613, cpwshop.com

AMENITIES: Hot showers, flush toilets, laundry, phone, vending machines

PARKING: At campsites or walk-in tent campers parking area

FEE: $9 Parks Pass, plus $18–$28 per night for walk-in tent sites; $26–$41 for others

ELEVATION: 7,000' at Elk Ridge; 6,600' at Pa-Co-Chu-Puk

RESTRICTIONS:

PETS: Must be leashed

QUIET HOURS: 10 p.m.–6 a.m.

FIRES: In fire rings only

ALCOHOL: Permitted

VEHICLES: On paved roads only

OTHER: 14-day stay limit

ranges; you'll appreciate the perspective from this elevation. There are two separate loops at Elk Ridge, both of which have electricity and are especially popular for tent campers. Check out Loop E to find a set of 10 walk-in tent campsites that will give you a slightly more remote feel—but with the luxury of carts to haul your stuff in.

The gravel path through this walk-in camping area goes beneath some gnarled old piñons, with separate short paths leading to each well-separated site. Three of the sites are near the edge of a precipice over the lake, so keep an eye on children and pets. Sites 151 and 153 offer the best views. All the sites have adequate shade trees and large, level tent pads for sound sleeping. Water spigots are located at the tent-campers parking area. There is a modern restroom amid the walk-in sites, though the showers and laundry are in the camper services building 100 or so yards distant. To reach a scenic overlook, take the 0.7-mile Sunset Ridge Trail and take in the views.

Pa-Co-Chu-Puk Campground, named for a Ute term meaning "cow creek," is located 3.5 miles north of the Dutch Charlie area. It has two loops that have water, bathrooms, and electricity, but they are out in the open and full of RVs. However, this campground also has a 15-site, walk-in tent camping loop that is across the Uncompahgre River from the rest of the park. This loop offers a more rustic experience yet is adjacent to the high-quality facilities that Ridgway offers. This loop is set in a ponderosa pine wood, complemented by Gambel oak and piñon pine, that gently rises up the slope below the Ridgway Dam.

Load your gear on a complimentary cart and cross the river to the tent camping area. Campsites are nestled here and there among the trees, and the river is clearly audible. At each site, the level picnic table and tent pad make your experience more comfortable without affecting the peaceful natural surroundings. Most of the sites are on the outside of the loop and are a decent distance from one another, making for a private and uncrowded experience. Site 282 is a favorite, with plenty of shade and soothing river sounds. The water spigot is near the parking area, and the showers are a good distance away, by the RV loops. Two quiet fishing ponds are nice for young anglers.

No matter where you are in this park, the first-rate facilities will spoil you. Recreational activities around here are first-rate too. Easy hiking and biking access on the natural-surface trails brings rewarding views. You can fish for trout or kokanee salmon in the reservoir, or try water-skiing, windsurfing, or sailing. The marina rents stand-up paddleboards, and the visitor center lends out fishing poles and tackle. The modern swim beach and playground are ideal for families with children.

The Uncompahgre River flows below the reservoir. You can catch and release fish on the river or keep the fish caught on nearby ponds. Hikers and bikers have 14 miles of trails to choose from to explore the park. Ranger-led hikes and programs inform campers about the natural resources of Ridgway. Check out the visitor center, too, as well as the Dallas Creek Nature Trail and the Oak Leaf Nature Trail, chock-full of information about the park's history and wildlife.

You would think such a fantastic state park would be constantly full. Not so. However, it does get busy around the major holidays and later in the summer. If you make it out here in September, the fall colors are sure to be out of this world.

Ridgway State Park Campgrounds

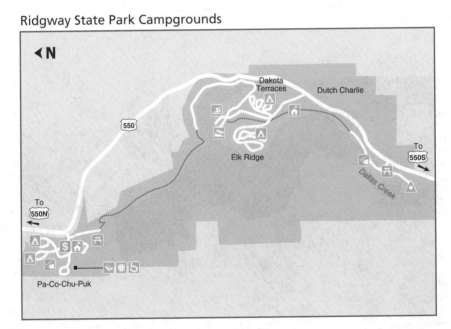

GETTING THERE

From Ridgway, drive north on US 550 for 5 miles to the Dutch Charlie entrance of the park, which will be on your left.

GPS COORDINATES: N38° 12.534' W107° 43.786'

47

⚕ Silver Jack Campground

Beauty: ★★★★★ / Privacy: ★★★★ / Spaciousness: ★★★ / Quiet: ★★★★ / Security: ★★★ / Cleanliness: ★★★★★

Stay among the aspens at the Uncompahgre National Forest's finest campground.

Silver Jack Campground is one of the prettiest campgrounds in one of the prettiest spots in the state. Located near the forks of the Cimarron River in the shadow of Uncompahgre Peak, the campground borders 2-mile-long Silver Jack Reservoir, which enhances the forests, meadows, and summits of the nearby Uncompahgre Wilderness. Only hand-propelled boats are allowed on the reservoir, maintaining peace and quiet to go along with the scenery both in and beyond the campground.

The campground is situated on a knoll above the lake, surrounded by aspens. Their leaves flutter in the wind to create an ever-changing mosaic of light on the forest floor. Tall grass forms an unbroken understory that contrasts with the white trunks of the aspen. This is the reason we tent campers do what we do.

Peeking through the aspens at Silver Jack Campground

KEY INFORMATION

LOCATION: Montrose

INFORMATION: U.S. Forest Service; Grand Mesa, Uncompahgre, and Gunnison National Forests; Ouray Ranger District; 970-240-5300; fs.usda.gov/gmug

OPEN: Mid June–early October

SITES: 60

EACH SITE HAS: Picnic table, fire grate

WHEELCHAIR ACCESS: No designated accessible sites

ASSIGNMENT: First come, first served; no reservations

REGISTRATION: Self-registration on-site

AMENITIES: Water, vault toilets

PARKING: At campsites only

FEE: $16 per night

ELEVATION: 9,000'

RESTRICTIONS:

PETS: Must be leashed

QUIET HOURS: None

FIRES: In fire grates only

ALCOHOL: At campsites only

VEHICLES: 30'

OTHER: 14-day stay limit

Silver Jack has three tiered loops. The roads are paved, as is each camper's parking spot, which is a nice touch after the long, bumpy, dusty road in. The first loop, Ouray, has a short two-way road with campsites along it before the actual loop starts. Ouray is at the lowest level and has 20 campsites set in the aspens. A small meadow breaks up the trees, along with an occasional small evergreen.

The Chipeta and Sapinero Loops may be closed in the early season or if the campground doesn't fill. Chipeta circles around a meadow of its own, yet all the campsites are in an extremely dense aspen wood. The young trees make for shady campsites and offer great privacy, especially on the upper section of this loop. This seems to be the most popular place to camp.

The Sapinero Loop is the highest on the knoll. If it's open, snag a spot here. The aspens are larger and allow more light to filter in so wildflowers thrive. The surrounding mountain views are better too. The road rolls upward, with campsites spread far apart, though they tighten up as the loop is completed.

Water spigots and exceptionally clean vault toilets are evenly spread about the campground. There should be no trouble finding a campsite in June, when the weather is less predictable and can still be chilly. When my family and I were there midweek in June, only the Ouray Loop was open, and we had it all to ourselves. In July and August, arrive early to ensure a campsite on weekends. September is a wonderful time to visit and watch the aspen leaves change color. Anytime is a great time to relax in this wonderful campground setting.

As for activities, hiking, fishing, and boating are the main attractions. An informal trail circles Silver Jack Reservoir, so you can bank fish for rainbow trout, brook trout, and kokanee salmon. By all means, if you have a canoe, bring it. Your arms are the only motor you can use here. The scenery from a boat in the middle of the lake is inspiring. A good second is the view from the Silver Jack Overlook just south of the campground.

Fly fishers like to try their luck on one of the three forks of the Cimarron River, as the waters tumble down from the wilderness above. Beaver Lake lies a mile below Silver Jack and is also popular for fishing (and camping, if you need an alternative spot). The smaller

Fish Creek reservoirs are just a few miles north of Silver Jack on Cimarron Road. No one swims in these chilly lakes.

Silver Jack derived its moniker from the mine of the same name located in the Uncompahgre Wilderness just south of the campground. You can hike up the East Fork Trail (#228) to the old mine site. Always be careful near any mine, closed or open. Beyond the mine site are two waterfalls of the East Fork.

You don't have to go to Europe to climb the Matterhorn. There's one right here in the Uncompahgre Wilderness. Take the Middle Fork Trail (#227) for a challenging day hike to top the 13,590-foot peak. Uncompahgre Peak is a fourteener, but it can't be reached in one day from this side of the wilderness.

For an easier hike, go to Cimarron Ridge, across the reservoir. It can be accessed from Trail #222. You'll end up at 10,800-foot Lou Creek Pass, overlooking your camping paradise. Or hike up to High Mesa on the Alpine Trail, which starts near the campground. Or you may just want to hang out and watch the aspens flutter in the wind.

Silver Jack Campground

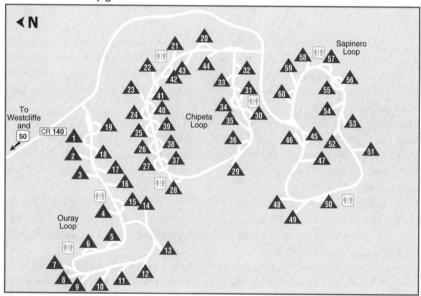

GETTING THERE

From Montrose, drive 23 miles east on US 50 to Cimarron Road. Turn right on Cimarron Road and follow it 21 miles to Silver Jack, which will be on your right.

GPS COORDINATES: N38° 14.048' W107° 32.283'

48

⚠ Amphitheater Campground

Beauty: ★★★★ / Privacy: ★★★★ / Spaciousness: ★★★ / Quiet: ★★★★ / Security: ★★★★ /
Cleanliness: ★★★★

Pitch your tent at this campground in the Switzerland of America, where you'll want to spend a few days soaking in the scenery, adventure, and local hot springs.

You won't find many campgrounds with a view quite like the one you'll get from Amphitheater Campground in Ouray. Ouray is named for Chief Ouray, a Ute leader in Colorado during the late 19th century. Situated on US 550 and part of the San Juan Skyway Scenic and Historic Byway, Ouray is among Colorado's most beautiful places. The mountains rise up in all directions, and the town itself is overflowing with charm.

Amphitheater Campground is named for the rock formations that form a natural circular gallery over the town. The massive gray cliffs are the result of ancient volcanic explosions and glacial movement. Perched on a mountainside, the campground showcases incredible views of these cliff faces and the town below.

View of Ouray from Amphitheater Campground

KEY INFORMATION

LOCATION: Ouray

INFORMATION: U.S. Forest Service; Grand Mesa, Uncompahgre, and Gunnison National Forests; Ouray Ranger District; 970-874-6600; fs.usda.gov/gmug

OPEN: June 10–Oct. 5

SITES: 35

EACH SITE HAS: Tent pad, fire ring, picnic tables

WHEELCHAIR ACCESS: Sites 16 and 17 are ADA-accessible.

ASSIGNMENT: First come, first served; no reservations

REGISTRATION: On-site

AMENITIES: Vault toilets, treated and pressurized water

PARKING: At campsites only

FEE: $24 per night

ELEVATION: 8,470'

RESTRICTIONS:

PETS: Must be leashed

QUIET HOURS: 10 p.m.–6 a.m.

FIRES: In fire rings only

ALCOHOL: Permitted

VEHICLES: 30'

OTHER: 14-day stay limit

To get to the campground, you'll leave town as though you're headed onto the Million Dollar Highway. Make a sharp left onto County Road 16, then stay left on Amphitheater Campground Road. You'll encounter Baby Bathtubs Trailhead, and shortly after, a pleasant picnic area with tables anchored on the slope among the trees.

Climbing the steep road to the campground can be intimidating, which is why the area is predominantly occupied by tents and small campers. (There are also no water, sewer, or electric hookups.) However, RVs can park at sites 3, 4, 16–18, 30, and 31, which you'll see if you take the second right and follow the TRAILER signs.

Instead, look for one of the designated tent-only sites. I especially liked site 33, near the campground entrance, as it was tucked away from the rest of the sites. In the farthest loop, sites 10–14 are all tent-only and offer a lovely and quiet camping experience. Just beyond sites 20 and 21 is a paved parking area with a stunning overlook. The campground host is usually stationed across from site 30. I'd stay away from sites 28 and 29 because of their lack of privacy. Most of the other sites are nicely shaded by the forest of Gambel oak trees and mixed conifers.

There are many excellent hiking trails in the immediate area. Perhaps the most popular is the Upper Cascade Falls Trail, which begins right at the campground and ends at the Chief Ouray Mine. You'll get incredible views of the amphitheater as well as Hayden Mountain and Potosi Peak, two thirteeners in the area. Baby Bathtubs Trail is another trail that begins at the bottom of Amphitheater Campground Road. It is a popular choice for families and a good connector to the Portland Trail and the Ice Park Trail. To see Ouray from all angles, hike the Perimeter Trail. This 6.5-mile loop begins across from the Ouray Visitor Center on the east side of US 550 (park behind the visitor center), but you can also hop on it from Box Canyon Falls, a great stop if you're into waterfalls.

Be sure to book enough time in Ouray to take advantage of the historic Ouray Hot Springs, a public facility open year-round. With geothermal soaking pools, cold-water pools, waterslides, and lap swimming, you can elevate your tent camping experience with a luxurious soak. A nice benefit is that there's no sulphur smell.

The campground is also a favorite among Jeep and off-road enthusiasts, as this area is known for off-road adventures. If you camp here, you can rent a Jeep in Ouray or go on a guided 4x4 tour of local ghost towns or scenic Imogene Pass.

Amphitheater Campground

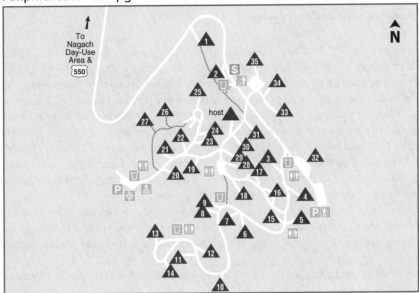

GETTING THERE

From the Ouray Visitor Center, travel south on US 550 for 1.8 miles. Turn left at the Amphitheater Campground sign and travel about 1 mile to the campground.

GPS COORDINATES: N38° 01.320' W107° 39.673'

49

⚠ Stone Cellar Campground

Beauty: ★★★★ / Privacy: ★★ / Spaciousness: ★★★★ / Quiet: ★★★★ / Security: ★★ / Cleanliness: ★★★

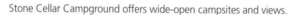

Stone Cellar is in the heart of 15,000-acre Saguache Park, the largest meadowland in the entire national forest system.

When you cross the Continental Divide at South Pass, Saguache (pronounced suh-WACH) Park opens up before you. It is an expanse of rolling, grassy terrain cut with creeks and bordered by massive peaks fringed in forestland. Smaller, lesser-used forest roads splinter off in all directions, beckoning you to see what lies over the next hill. Farther down, along the Middle Fork of Saguache Creek, lies the Stone Cellar Campground. Beyond the campground, open parkland rolls on to the La Garita Mountains and the La Garita Wilderness.

The La Garita Wilderness looks over more meadowlands, as well as old-growth forests and trout-laden streams and lakes (*La Garita* means "the lookout"). There are more than 120,000 acres and 175 miles of trails to enjoy in this seldom visited slice of wild Colorado. The Wheeler Geologic Area is also within the wilderness.

Arriving at this campground, you will immediately notice a lack of trees. Middle Fork flows out of a meadow from above into a canyon down below, vertical rock walls rise up at the campground, and the views of the distant mountains inspire a different type of camping experience.

A wooden stock fence surrounds a handful of the campsites here. The campground lies alongside a working cow camp with real cowboys at work during the summer months. The other sites border the gurgling Saguache Creek. There is a vault toilet but no water. One

Stone Cellar Campground offers wide-open campsites and views.

U.S. Forest Service

LOCATION: Saguache

INFORMATION: U.S. Forest Service, Rio Grande National Forest, Saguache Ranger District; 719-655-2547; fs.usda.gov/riogrande

OPEN: Memorial Day–Labor Day

SITES: 6

EACH SITE HAS: Picnic table, fire ring

WHEELCHAIR ACCESS: No designated accessible sites

ASSIGNMENT: First come, first served; no reservations

REGISTRATION: Not needed

AMENITIES: Vault toilet; no water or trash collection

PARKING: At campsites only

FEE: $5 per night

ELEVATION: 9,500'

RESTRICTIONS:

PETS: Must be leashed

QUIET HOURS: None

FIRES: In fire rings only

ALCOHOL: At campsites only

VEHICLES: 25'

OTHER: 14-day stay limit

ranger told me that campers are welcome to stop at the Saguache Park Ranger office for water during operating hours during the week. Otherwise, be sure to pack it in and pack it out. The wide-open meadow affords campers wonderful views, and fishing in the Saguache Creek is excellent, with plentiful rainbow, brown, and cutthroat trout.

Saguache Park deserves a visit, especially later in the summer when the whole place is awash in wildflowers. For more wooded camping options, Luders Creek Campground offers pleasant shaded spots with Engelmann spruce and quaking aspen groves. Dispersed camping at Salt House (about a mile north on the road you came in on) is another desirable spot with good views of the area.

Another option is the Stone Cellar Guard Station Cabin, a remote cabin offering solitude and seclusion just outside the boundary to the La Garita Wilderness area in Saguache Park, about a half mile west of the campground. The rustic cabin makes a great fishing or big-game hunting camp in the fall months.

Farther up County Road 17FF beyond the campground is the South Saguache Trail. It starts at 10,400 feet and follows the creek for good fishing and easy access to the high country toward Half Moon Pass. Whale Creek Trail starts here, too, and heads toward Palmer Mesa.

FS 744, which turns off right before the campground and has the one lonesome campsite, leads farther up the Middle Fork of Saguache Creek to another trailhead. Here you can walk to the headwaters of the Saguache and into lake country. Half Moon Pass Trail starts here too; it's a 7-mile, one-way hike to the Wheeler Geologic Area but can be done in a single day. If you leave early in the morning, you will have time to view the area and still return by nightfall.

The North Fork Saguache has its own trail to headwaters made up of several small tributaries; a few beaver ponds are scattered along the way. This trail is outside the wilderness and can be accessed by FS 776. This is a place to take in the view, cast a fishing line, and get an eyeful of Saguache Park.

Stone Cellar Campground

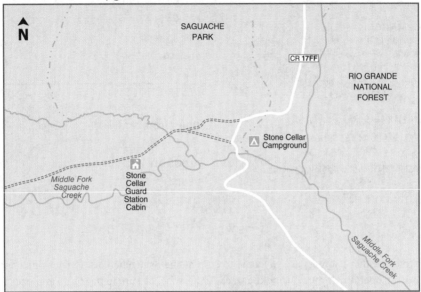

GETTING THERE

From Saguache, go 35 miles west on CO 114. Turn left on County Road 17GG and travel 6 miles. Turn left on CR NN14, then right on CR 17FF. Proceed 13 miles to Stone Cellar Campground.

GPS COORDINATES: N38° 01.205' W106° 40.700'

⚲ Transfer Park Campground

Beauty: ★★★★★ / Privacy: ★★★★ / Spaciousness: ★★★★ / Quiet: ★★★ / Security: ★★★ /
Cleanliness: ★★★★

Make a transfer to the most attractive campground in the San Juan National Forest.

Transfer Park is steeped in history. The attractive, mountain-rimmed meadow was once a point where tools and supplies were transferred from horse-drawn wagons to mules for use beyond the rugged Florida River canyon in the late 1800s. Ore, mostly gold and silver, would be brought down in the wagons. These days, the 11-acre site is such a scenic campground that it may be hard to pull yourself away to enjoy the hiking, fishing, rafting, train riding, and town touring the area has to offer.

Veer left past the popular Florida Campground, and look for the sign for the entrance to Transfer Park Campground. There are two loops, the south loop and the north loop. The south loop has 10 campsites and is set in a mature aspen grove mixed with some ponderosa

You can find any combination of sun and shade you like at Transfer Park Campground.

KEY INFORMATION

LOCATION: Durango

INFORMATION: U.S. Forest Service, San Juan National Forest, Columbine Ranger District; 970-884-2512; fs.usda.gov/sanjuan

OPEN: May 1–mid-September

SITES: 25

EACH SITE HAS: Picnic table, fire grate

WHEELCHAIR ACCESS: No designated accessible sites

ASSIGNMENT: First come, first served no reservations

REGISTRATION: With camp host

AMENITIES: Water, vault toilets, trash collection

PARKING: At campsites only

FEE: $20 per night

ELEVATION: 8,600'

RESTRICTIONS:

PETS: Must be leashed

QUIET HOURS: 10 p.m.–6 a.m.

FIRES: In fire grates only

ALCOHOL: At campsites only

VEHICLES: 35'

OTHER: 14-day stay limit

pine, Douglas-fir, and small clearings. Smaller trees and brush form the understory. The campsites are large and well separated from one another. Wooden posts delineate the sites. The forest closes near the meadow then opens back up as the loop is completed. You can find just about any combination of sun and shade you desire. There is one vault toilet and one spigot on this loop.

The north loop is closer to the Florida River. Although some sites are more in the meadow than others, the thicker forest and rock outcrops make for a closed-in, intimate feeling on this loop. The Florida River provides the best kind of white noise. About half the campsites are on the heavily wooded inner loop. A few campsites and a wooden fence border the river gorge. Site 21 is a large double site at the top of the loop that makes a prime spot for a larger group. Sites 16, 17, and 18 are especially desirable if you like camping by a river. Two vault toilets and two water spigots serve this loop.

This campground rarely fills up, although when I was there, a gaggle of folks drove in just to dip their toes into a frigid river eddy just across the meadow. Some trailers and RVs do make it here, but its spread-out sites and proximity to the river make it a haven for tent campers.

Those who do come here get to choose among an array of nearby activities. Fish the Florida River for a chance at catching rainbow and brown trout. Hiking comes naturally on the Burnt Timber Trail (667), which starts about a mile north of the campground and leads into the nearly 500,000-acre Weminuche Wilderness (no mountain bikes or motorized vehicles allowed). The trail offers connections to Lime Mesa, Mountain View Crest, and City Reservoir. You can hitch your horses in the parking area, but horses are not allowed in the campground.

Just up bumpy Forest Service Road (FS) 597, which starts by Florida Campground, are two short hikes into Lost Lake and Stump Lake. For great fishing and nonmotorized boating opportunities, head downstream from Transfer Park to Lemon Reservoir. The popular angling areas are near the dam and at the Lemon Day Use Area.

The rest of the action is down Durango way. Durango is a historic Western town that is cashing in on the tourism craze. Spend some time in the charming town, and if you want to take a ride through some good natural scenery, try the narrow-gauge Silverton Train (durangotrain.com). The Durango & Silverton Railroad was constructed in the 1880s to haul gold and silver from the San Juan Mountains. The train trip is a great way to see the Weminuche Wilderness. It is an all-day affair getting to and from Silverton, but it promises a scenic trip and memories for a lifetime.

The rivers offer more rollicking action. The Lower Animas offers milder Class III rapids through Durango, great for families with children. The Upper Animas is more extreme, with Class IV–V rapids. The Piedra River is another source of Class II, III, and IV rafting fun. Contact one of the many outfitters in Durango to book your adventure.

Transfer Park Campground

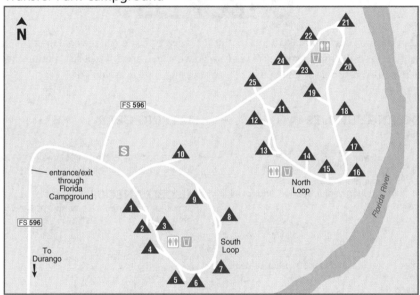

GETTING THERE

From Durango, take CR 240 (Florida Road) north 14 miles to CR 243. Stay left on CR 243, and drive 7 miles, passing Lemon Reservoir. Turn left on FS 596, passing through Florida Campground and veering left to arrive at Transfer Park in 1 mile.

GPS COORDINATES: N37° 27.772' W107° 40.782'

APPENDIX A

CAMPING EQUIPMENT CHECKLIST

Except for the large and bulky items on this list, keep a plastic storage container full of the essentials for car camping so they're ready to go when you are. Make a last-minute check of the inventory, resupply anything that's low or missing, and away you go.

COOKING SUPPLIES
Bottle opener
Can opener
Cast iron pot with lid
Corkscrew
Cups (plastic or aluminum)
Dish soap (biodegradable), sponge, and towel
Flatware
Foil
Food of your choice
Frying pan and spatula
Ice
Lighter and/or matches in waterproof container
Plates
Pocketknife
Salt, pepper, spices, sugar, coffee, tea, and cooking oil and maple syrup in waterproof, spillproof containers
Stove and fuel
Wooden spoon

FIRST AID KIT
Adhesive bandages
Antibiotic ointment (Neosporin or generic equivalent)
Antiseptic or disinfectant, such as Betadine or hydrogen peroxide
Aspirin or acetaminophen
Benadryl or generic equivalent, diphenhydramine (for allergic reactions)
Butterfly-closure bandages
Epinephrine autoinjector (for severe allergic reactions to bee stings)
Gauze roll and pads
Moleskin or Spenco 2nd Skin
Tweezers
Waterproof first aid tape

SLEEPING GEAR
Pillow
Sleeping bag
Sleeping pad (inflatable or insulated)
Tent with ground tarp and rainfly

MISCELLANEOUS
Bath soap (biodegradable), washcloth, and towel
Camp chair
Cooler
Deck of cards/books
Flashlight/headlamp
Hand sanitizer
Lanterns
Paper towels and toilet paper
Plastic ziplock bags
Shovel
Sunglasses, hat, and sunscreen
Warm clothes, raingear, and hiking boots
Water bottle
Wool blanket

OPTIONAL
Barbecue grill
Binoculars
Cell phone
Compass
Day pack for hiking
Field guides
Fishing rod and tackle
GPS device
Maps (road, trail, topographic, etc.)

APPENDIX B

SOURCES OF INFORMATION

The following is a partial list of agencies, associations, and organizations to contact for information on outdoor recreation opportunities in Colorado.

U.S. BUREAU OF LAND MANAGEMENT

Little Snake Field Office
970-826-5000
blm.gov/office/little-snake-field-office

COLORADO PARKS & WILDLIFE

cpw.state.co.us

Arkansas Headwater Recreation Area
719-539-7289, ahra@state.co.us

Golden Gate Canyon State Park
303-582-3707, dnr_goldengatepark@state.co.us

Jackson Lake State Park
970-645-2551, jackson.lake@state.co.us

Mueller State Park Campground
719-687-2366, mueller.park@state.co.us

Pearl Lake State Park Campground
970-879-3922, steamboat.lake@state.co.us

Ridgway State Park
970-626-5822

Rifle Falls State Park Campground
970-625-1607, rifle.gap.park@state.co.us

South Republican State Wildlife Area
719-227-5200

State Forest
970-723-8366, state.forest@state.co.us

Staunton State Park Campground
303-816-0912, staunton.park@state.co.us

LARIMER COUNTY PARKS AND OPEN LANDS DEPARTMENT

970-619-4570, parksoffice@larimer.org
larimer.org/naturalresources/parks

NATIONAL PARK SERVICE

Black Canyon of the Gunnison National Park
970-641-2337, nps.gov/blca

Colorado National Monument
970-858-3617, ext 360; nps.gov/colm

Curecanti National Recreation Area
970-641-2337, ext. 205; nps.gov/cure

Dinosaur National Monument
970-374-3000 or 435-781-7700, nps.gov/dino

Great Sand Dunes National Monument
719-378-6300, nps.gov/grsa

Rocky Mountain National Park
970-586-1206, nps.gov/romo

U.S. FOREST SERVICE

ARAPAHO & ROOSEVELT NATIONAL FORESTS AND PAWNEE NATIONAL GRASSLAND
fs.usda.gov/arp

> **Boulder Ranger District**
> 303-541-2500
>
> **Canyon Lakes Ranger District**
> 970-295-6700, sm.fs.canyonlakes@usda.gov
>
> **Sulphur Ranger District**
> 970-887-4100, sm.fs.sulphur@usda.gov
>
> **Divide Ranger District**
> 719-657-3321

GRAND MESA, UNCOMPAHGRE, AND GUNNISON NATIONAL FORESTS
fs.usda.gov/gmug

> **Grand Valley Ranger District**
> 970-242-8211
>
> **Supervisor's Office**
> 970-874-6600, sm.fs.r2gmuginfo@usda.gov
>
> **Gunnison Ranger District**
> 970-641-0471
>
> **Ouray Ranger District**
> 970-240-5300
>
> **Paonia Ranger District**
> 970-527-4131

MEDICINE BOW–ROUTT NATIONAL FORESTS, THUNDER BASIN NATIONAL GRASSLAND
fs.usda.gov/mbt

Yampa Ranger District
970-638-4516

PIKE AND SAN ISABEL NATIONAL FORESTS, CIMARRON AND COMANCHE NATIONAL GRASSLANDS
fs.usda.gov/psicc

Salida Ranger District
719-539-3591

Forest Supervisor Office
719-553-1400

Leadville Ranger District
719-486-0749

San Carlos Ranger District
719-269-8500

South Platte Ranger District
303-275-5610

RIO GRANDE NATIONAL FOREST
fs.usda.gov/riogrande

Conejos Peak Ranger District
719-274-8971

Saguache Ranger District
719-655-2547

SAN JUAN NATIONAL FOREST
fs.usda/gov/sanjuan

Dolores Ranger District
970-882-7296

Pagosa Ranger District
970-264-2268

Columbine Ranger District
970-884-2512

WHITE RIVER NATIONAL FOREST
fs.usda.gov/whiteriver

Blanco Ranger District
970-878-4039

Eagle Ranger District
970-328-6388

Holy Cross Ranger District
970-827-5715

ROYAL GORGE REGION
royalgorgeregion.com/camping

Cañon City Chamber of Commerce
719-275-2331

INDEX

A

Abyss Lake, 47
Alpine Lodge, Alvarado Campground, 111
altitude sickness, 3
Alvarado Campground, 109–111
American Lakes, 32
Amphitheater Campground, 161–163
animal hazards, 4–6, 7
Animas River, 169
Arapaho Glacier, 66–67
Arapaho National Forest, 46
Arapaho National Wildlife Refuge, 33
Arkansas River, 119, 121
Aspen Meadow Campground, Golden Gate
    Canyon State Park, 43–44, 45
Aspenglen Campground, Rocky Mountain
    National Park, 71–73

B

backcountry camping, 8–9
    Black Canyon of the Gunnison National
        Park, 136
    Colorado National Monument, 85
    Golden Gate Canyon State Park, 44
    Mueller State Park Campground, 125
bathrooms. See toileting
Bear Lake Campground, 112–114
Bear River, 81, 83
bears, 4–5, 9
beauty rating, 1
Beaver Lake, 159
Beckwith Pass, 144
Berthoud Pass, 68, 70
Big Thompson Canyon Road, 37
bighorn sheep, 56
Black Canyon of the Gunnison National Park:
    North Rim Campground, 134–136
Blue Lake, 113–114
Bonnett Creek, 114
Bonny Lake, 24, 25
Browns Park, 93, 94
Browns Park Campground, 28–30
Browns Park National Wildlife Refuge, 93, 95
Buffalo Campground, 28–30
Buffalo Creek, 29
Buffalo Peaks Wilderness, 74, 75
Burro Bridge Campground, 137–139

C

Cache La Poudre River, 58–59
Calypso Cascades, 54
Cameron Pass, 32
Camp Dick Campground, 61–64
campgrounds. See also specific campground
    best-rated, ix–x
    Eastern Colorado, 13–26
    GPS coordinates, 2
    hike-in sites, 44, 78
    layout maps and legend, xi, 2
    North Central Colorado, 27–79
    Northwest Colorado, 80–107
    profiles and rating system, 1–2
    South Central Colorado, 108–132
    Southwest Colorado, 133–161
    wilderness excursions from, tips on, 9
camping
    backcountry. See backcountry camping
    with children, 10–12
    dispersed. See dispersed camping areas
    with dogs, 12
    equipment checklist, 170
    etiquette, 7
    tips for happy trips, 7–8
Carhart, Arthur, 99
Carson, Kit, 20
Carter Lake, 38
Cassidy, Butch, 93
Cathedral Campground, 140–142
Cathedral Creek, 141
Cathedral Rock, 140, 141
Champion Mine, 35
Chapin Mesa, 150, 151
checklists
    camping equipment, 170
    first aid kit contents, 4
Chief Ouray Mine, 162
children, camping with, 10–12
Cimarron Ridge, 160
Cimarron River, 158, 159
cleanliness rating, 2
    top five campgrounds, ix

C *(continued)*
Clear Lake, 32
cliff dwellings, 149, 150–151
climate overview, 3
clothing, 8
Cold Spring Mountain, 93, 94
Cold Springs Campground, 81–83
Collegiate Peaks, 121
Colorado Gold Medal Waters, 134, 142
Colorado National Monument: Saddlehorn
        Campground, 84–86
Colorado Parks & Wildlife (contact information), 171
Colorado River, 70, 84
Colorado State Forest, 32
Colorado Trail, 28, 29, 34, 35, 56
Comanche Lake, 110, 111
Comanche Peaks Wilderness, 59
Continental Divide Trail, 122, 131–132, 147
Copeland Falls, 54
CORSAR search-and-rescue card, 4
COTREX (Colorado Trail Explorer) app, 56–57
Coulter Mesa, 98
Crag Crest National Recreation Trail, 106
The Crags Campground, 31–33
Craig Creek, 29, 56
Craig Peak, 90, 92
Crestone, 129
Cripple Creek, 126
Crow Valley Family Campground, Pawnee National
        Grassland, 21–23
Cumbres and Toltec Scenic Railroad, 130, 132
Cumbres Pass, 130, 132

D
Dallas Creek Project/Recreation Site, 155
Deadhorse Gulch, 136
Devils Causeway, 83
Dinosaur National Monument: Echo Park
        Campground, 87–89
Dinosaur Quarry Visitor Center Museum, 89
dispersed camping areas
    East Ridge Campground, 118, 119
    Guanella Pass Campground, 48
    Pawnee Buttes, 22
    Rio Grande National Forest, 129, 131, 165
    Robbers Roost Campground, 68
    South Republican State Wildlife Area, 24–26
dogs, camping with, 12
Dollar Lake, 145
Dome Rock, 126
drinking water, 9, 10, 12
Dude's Fishing Hole, 44
Durango, 168–169
Durango & Silverton Railroad, 169

E
East Beckwith Mountains, 143
East Brush Creek, 90
East Fork Rifle Creek, 97
East Lost Park, 56
East Ridge Campground, 118–120
East Willow Creek, 152, 153
Echo Park Campground, Dinosaur National
        Monument, 87–89
Elbert Creek Campground, 34–36
Embargo Creek, 141
Emerald Lake, 36
emergencies
    first aid kits, 4
    getting lost, 9
    hypothermia, 9
    search-and-rescue cards for, 4
Encampment River, 104
equipment checklist, 170
Estes Park, 37, 50
etiquette, camping, 7

F
Fancy Lake, 41
Far View Lodge, Mesa Verde National Park, 150
first aid kits, 4, 170
Fish Creek reservoirs, 160
Flat Tops Wilderness, 82, 83, 100
Flatiron Lake, 38
Florida River, 168
food, 8, 9
Four-Mile Day Use Area, Mueller State Park, 126
Fraser Creek, 100
Fraser River, 70
Frazer Meadow, 44
Fulford Cave Campground, 90–92

G
Gates of Lodore, 93, 94
Gold Park Campground, 40–42
Gold Park Mining Company, 41
Golden Gate Canyon State Park Campgrounds,
        43–45
GPS coordinates for campgrounds, 2
Grand Lake, 69
Grand Mesa, 105, 106
Grays Creek, 122
Great Sand Dunes National Park & Preserve:
        Piñon Flats Campground, 115–117
Green River, 87, 88, 94
Grouse Mountain, 125
Guanella Pass Campground, 46–48
Gunnison River, Black Canyon of the, 134–135

H

Hahn's Peak, 102, 104
Halfmoon Creek, 34
Harpers Corner Scenic Drive, 89
Harvey Gap State Park, 98
Hayden Mountain, 162
hazards, 4–7, 8, 9
Heart Lake, 147
Hermit Lake, 111
Hermit Park Open Space: Hermit's Hollow
    Campground, 49–51
Highway of Legends Scenic and Historic
    Byway, 114
hike-in campsites, 44, 78
Holy Cross City, 40, 41
Holy Cross Wilderness, 40, 41, 91
Homestake Creek, 40
Houseman Park, 29
Hunky Dory Lake, 41
hypothermia, 9

I

Independence Monument, 85
Indian Peaks Wilderness, 61, 62, 65, 66–67
Irish Canyon Campground, 93–95
Iron Mike Mine, 36

J

Jackson Lake State Park Campground, 14–16
John Martin Reservoir State Wildlife Area, 17–20

K

Kelly Lake, 32
Kenosha Mountain, 55
Kruger Rock Trail, 49, 50

L

La Garita Mountain, 140
La Garita Wilderness, 164, 165
Lake Agnes, 32
Lake Charles, 92
Lake Hasty Campground, John Martin Reservoir
    State Wildlife Area, 18–19
lakeside camping, best campgrounds for, x
Larimer County Parks and Open Lands Dept.
    (contact information), 171
Leadville National Fish Hatchery, 36
Lemon Reservoir, 168
Leon Lake, 106
Leon Peak Reservoir, 106
lightning, 3

Lizard Head Wilderness, 137, 138–139
Lodore Hall, 93, 95
Longs Peak Campground, Rocky Mountain
    National Park, 52–54
lost, getting, 9
Lost Creek Wilderness, 29, 56
Lost Lake Campground, 143–145
Lost Lake Slough, 143, 144, 145
Lost Park Campground, 55–57
Lost Trail Campground, 146–148
Lower Laramie River valley, 28
Lower Narrows Campground, 58–60

M

Mancos Valley, 149
maps, campground
    layout and legend, xi, 2.
        See also specific campground
    locator, v
Marshall Pass, 122
Mary Jane ski area, 69
Medano Creek, 116, 117
Medicine Bow Mountains, 32
Mesa Verde National Park: Morefield Campground,
    149–151
Middle Saint Vrain Creek, 62–64
Mirror Lake Campground, 152–154
moose, 5, 31, 33
Moraine Park Museum, 53
Morefield Campground, Mesa Verde National Park,
    149–151
Mosquito Lake, 82
mosquitoes, 7
Mount Bierstadt, 47
Mount Champion Mill, 34
Mount Elbert, 34, 35
Mount Evans Wilderness, 46, 47
Mount Massive Wilderness, 34, 35
Mount Whitney, 42
Mount Zirkel Wilderness, 102, 104
mountain lions, 5
Mueller State Park Campground, 124–126
Mystic Island Lake, 92

N

Narrows Campgrounds, The, 58–60
National Park Service, 171 (contact information)
Naylor Lake, 47
Never Summer Mountains, 31
Nokhu Crags, 31, 32
North Crestone Creek Campground, 127–129
North Crestone Lake, 128–129
North Fork Elk River, 104

N *(Continued)*
North Michigan Reservoir, 32
North Park, 31, 33
North Rim Campground, Black Canyon of the
    Gunnison National Park, 134–136

O

O'Haver Lake Campground, 121–123
Otto, Jim, 84
Ouray, 161, 162
Ouray Hot Springs, 162
Ouzel Falls, 54
overlooks, safety at, 9

P

packing, for camping, 8, 10, 11
Pawnee Buttes, 22
Pawnee National Grassland: Crow Valley Family
    Campground, 21–23
Peaceful Valley Campground, 61–64
Peak to Peak Scenic Byway, 66–67
Pearl Lake, 102–103
Pearl Lake State Park Campground, 102–104
permits, 7, 47
petroglyphs, 20, 87, 88, 93, 94, 95
Piedra River, 169
Pike, Zebulon, 20
Pike National Forest, 28, 29
Pikes Peak, 124
Pinewood Reservoir Campground, 37–39
Piñon Flats Campground, Great Sand Dunes
    National Park & Preserve, 115–117
The Point Campground, John Martin Reservoir
    State Wildlife Area, 19–20
poison ivy, 6, 135
Potosi Peak, 162
Poudre River, 58–59
privacy rating, 1
    top five campgrounds, ix
profiles, campground, 1–2
Pueblo cliff dwellings, 149, 150–151

Q

quiet rating, 2
    top five campgrounds, ix

R

Raggeds Wilderness, 143, 144
Rainbow Lakes Campground, 65–67
Ramsay-Shockey Open Space, 38
ranger districts (contact information), 171–172

Ranger Lakes, 32
rating system, campground, 1–2
Rawah Wilderness, 28, 29
reservations, campground, vii, 8
Reverend's Ridge Campground, Golden Gate
    Canyon State Park, 43, 44, 45
Ridgeway State Park Campground, 155–157
Rifle Falls State Park Campground, 96–98
Rifle Gap State Park, 98
Rifle Mountain Park, 98
Rio Grande National Forest, 128, 130
Rio Grande Reservoir, 147
Rio Grande River, 141–142, 147
Rio Grande Southern Railroad, 139
Road Canyon Reservoir, 147
Robbers Roost Campground, 68–70
Rocky Mountain National Park, 31, 37, 50, 54, 61,
    62, 65, 66
    campgrounds in, 52–54, 71–73
Roosevelt National Forest, 46, 53
Routt National Forest, 104
Royal Gorge Bridge, 118, 119
Royal Gorge region (contact information), 172
Ruby Jewel Lake, 32

S

Sackett Reservoir, 106
Saddlehorn Campground, Colorado National
    Monument, 84–86
Saguache Creek, 164, 165
Saguache Park, 164–166
Salida, 121
San Juan Mountains, 130, 132, 146, 149, 169
San Luis Lakes State Park, 117
Sand Wash Basin, 94
Sangre de Cristo Mountains/Wilderness,
    109–114, 117, 128
Santa Fe Trail, 20
search-and-rescue cards, 4
security rating, 2
    top five campgrounds, ix
Seven Sisters Lakes, 41
Shadow Mountain Lake, 69
Shepherds Rim Campground, 99–101
Silver Dollar Lake, 47
Silver Jack Campground, 158–160
Silver Jack Reservoir, 158, 159
sleeping bags/gear, 8, 270
snakes, 6
Snow Lake, 32
South Crestone Lake, 129
South Platte River, 75
South Republican State Wildlife Area
    campgrounds, 24–26

South San Juan Wilderness, 130, 131–132
spaciousness rating, 2
 top five campgrounds, ix
Spanish Peaks, 112
Staunton family, 77
Staunton State Park Campground, 77–79
Steamboat Lake, 102, 103, 104
Steamboat Lake State Park, 102–103
Steamboat Springs, 102
Stillwater Dam/Reservoir, 82, 83
Stone Cellar Campground, 164–166
Stoner Mesa, 139

T

Tarryall Mountain, 55
Taylor Mesa, 139
Taylor Reservoir, 153
temperatures, Denver area, 3
tents, pitching/staking, 7, 8
ticks, 6
Timber Creek Campground, 72
Tincup Pass, 153
toileting
 dog waste, 12
 human waste, 9
 at night, 8
tornadoes, 3
Tour of the Moon cycling event, 86
Trail Ridge Road, 53, 72
Transfer Park Campground, 167–169
Trappers Lake, 99–100
Treasure Vault Lake, 41
trees, dead/damaged, 8
Trinchera Peak, 114
Trujillo Meadows Campground, 130–132
Trujillo Meadows Reservoir, 130, 131

U

Uncompahgre Peak/Wilderness, 158, 160
Uncompahgre River, 157
U.S. Bureau of Land Management
 (contact information), 171
U.S. Forest Service (contact information),
 171–172

V

Venable Falls/Lakes, 110, 111
Venable Pass, 128
Vermillion Falls, 93, 94
Victor, 126
views, best campgrounds for, x

W

Wall Lake, 100, 101
water, drinking, 9, 10, 12
weather, 3
Weir and Johnson Campground, 105–107
Wellington Lake, 29
Weminuche Wilderness, 147, 168, 169
West Beckwith Mountains, 143
West Dolores River, 137
West Elk Wilderness, 143, 145
West Nile virus, 7
Westcliffe, 111
Weston Pass Campground, 74–76
Wet Mountain Valley, 109
Wetherill Mesa, 150, 151
wheelchair accessibility, best campgrounds for,
 x, 78
Wheeler Geologic Area, 165
Whispering Cave, Dinosaur National
 Monument, 88
White River, 100
White River National Forest, 98
Whitney Lake Trail, 42
Wild Basin: Rocky Mountain National Park, 54, 67
Wilderness Act of 1964, 99
Willow Lake, 129
Winter Park ski area, 69

Y

Yampa River, 87, 94
Yeoman Park, 90

Z

Zapata Falls, 117

ABOUT THE AUTHORS

Melissa Markle

Monica Parpal Stockbridge is a writer and editor born and raised in Colorado. She attended college in Omaha, Nebraska, but always knew she wanted to end up back in the Centennial State. Although she grew up hiking at state parks and snowboarding in the mountains, she didn't become a tent camper until adulthood when she started climbing fourteeners with friends. Now, she can proudly pitch her own tent and cook a damn good camp dinner on her Coleman stove. She hopes to share many more camping memories with her husband and young daughter.

Monica has written for numerous local, national, and international publications, including *The Denver Post, Colorado Traveler Magazine, 5280, Colorado Parent, ColoradoBiz,* and *Preferred Travel.* She contributed to the *Moon Denver, Boulder & Colorado Springs* guidebook. Today, she writes about travel and technology from her home in Denver.

For more about Monica, visit monicastockbridge.com.

Jacqueline Parpal (left) and Eleanor Stockbridge (right)

Johnny Molloy is an outdoor writer based in Johnson City, Tennessee. Born in Memphis, he moved to Knoxville in 1980 to attend the University of Tennessee. During his college years, he developed a love of the natural world that would lead him to backpack and canoe-camp throughout the United States over the next 25 years.

After graduating from UT with a degree in economics, Johnny spent an ever-increasing amount of time in the wild, becoming more skilled in a variety of environments. Friends enjoyed his adventure stories; one even suggested that he write a book. He pursued that idea and soon parlayed his love of the outdoors into an occupation.

Keri Anne Molloy

The results of his efforts are more than 40 books. These include hiking, camping, paddling, and other comprehensive guidebooks, as well as books on true outdoor adventures. Johnny has also written for numerous publications and websites. For the latest on Johnny, please visit johnnymolloy.com.

Courtesy of Kim Lipker

Kim Lipker grew up in Colorado loving the outdoors from an early age. She is the author of three other guidebooks for Menasha Ridge Press, *60 Hikes Within 60 Miles: Denver and Boulder, Day & Overnight Hikes in Rocky Mountain National Park,* and *Smart and Savvy Hiking for Women.* She also wrote *The Unofficial Guide to Bed & Breakfasts and Country Inns in the Rockies* (Hungry Minds).

DEAR CUSTOMERS AND FRIENDS,

SUPPORTING YOUR INTEREST IN OUTDOOR ADVENTURE, travel, and an active lifestyle is central to our operations, from the authors we choose to the locations we detail to the way we design our books. Menasha Ridge Press was incorporated in 1982 by a group of veteran outdoorsmen and professional outfitters. For many years now, we've specialized in creating books that benefit the outdoors enthusiast.

Almost immediately, Menasha Ridge Press earned a reputation for revolutionizing outdoors- and travel-guidebook publishing. For such activities as canoeing, kayaking, hiking, backpacking, and mountain biking, we established new standards of quality that transformed the whole genre, resulting in outdoor-recreation guides of great sophistication and solid content. Menasha Ridge Press continues to be outdoor publishing's greatest innovator.

The folks at Menasha Ridge Press are as at home on a whitewater river or mountain trail as they are editing a manuscript. The books we build for you are the best they can be, because we're responding to your needs. Plus, we use and depend on them ourselves.

We look forward to seeing you on the river or the trail. If you'd like to contact us directly, visit us at menasharidge.com. We thank you for your interest in our books and the natural world around us all.

SAFE TRAVELS,

Bob Sehlinger

BOB SEHLINGER
PUBLISHER